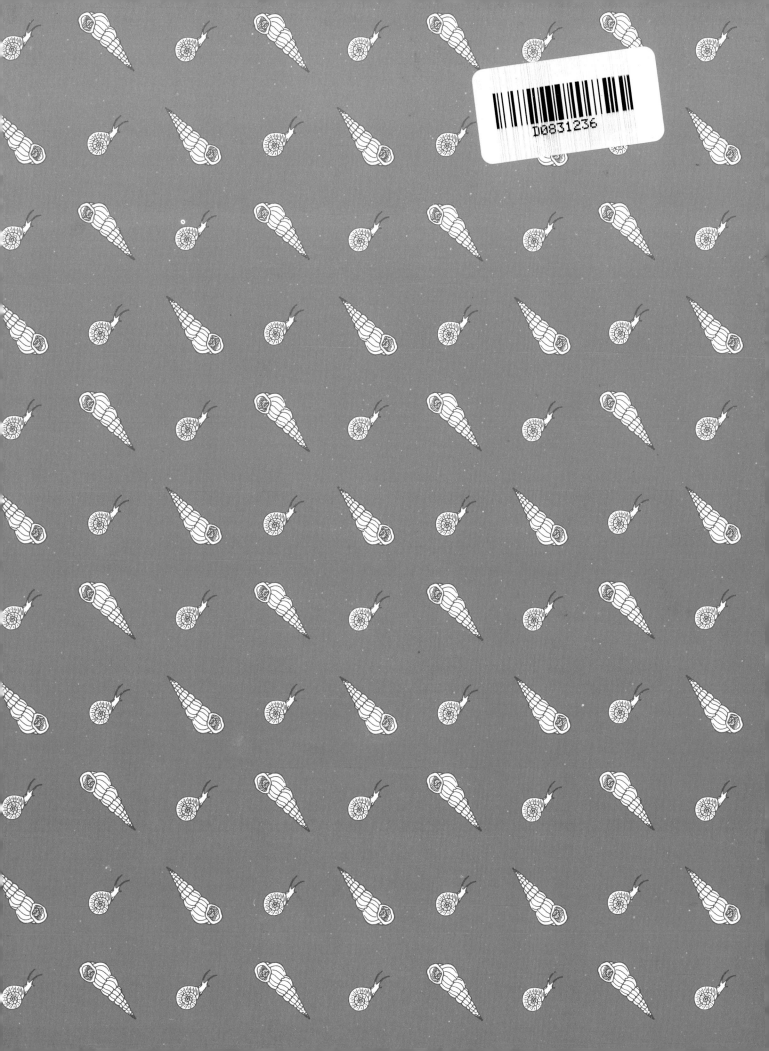

EYEWITNESS GUIDES

SHELL

Silver cross
inlaid with
abalone shell

Green
abalone

Oyster shell
with mussel

Freshwater
bivalve

Victor Dan's
delphinula
shell

Juvenile pen-
shell

Jamaican land
snails

Fossil
ammonite

Claw of European
edible crab

Polygyratia
land snail
shell

Angular crab

Community of
mollusc worm
tubes

Cuban land snails

Lamellose wentletraps

Precious wentletrap

EYEWITNESS ◉ GUIDES

SHELL

Written by
Alex Arthur

Venus comb murex

Japanese wonder shell

Cidaris sea urchin

Slate-pencil sea urchin

Baby hawksbill turtle

DORLING KINDERSLEY • LONDON

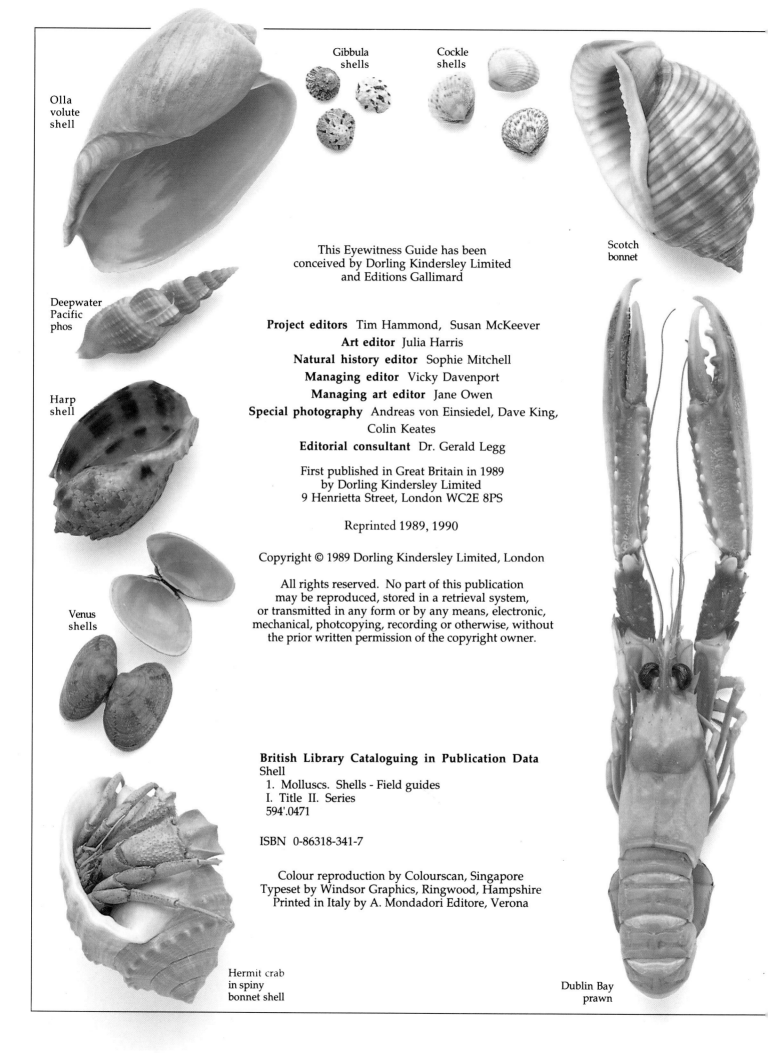

Olla volute shell

Gibbula shells

Cockle shells

Scotch bonnet

Deepwater Pacific phos

Harp shell

Venus shells

Hermit crab in spiny bonnet shell

Dublin Bay prawn

This Eyewitness Guide has been conceived by Dorling Kindersley Limited and Editions Gallimard

Project editors Tim Hammond, Susan McKeever
Art editor Julia Harris
Natural history editor Sophie Mitchell
Managing editor Vicky Davenport
Managing art editor Jane Owen
Special photography Andreas von Einsiedel, Dave King, Colin Keates
Editorial consultant Dr. Gerald Legg

First published in Great Britain in 1989 by Dorling Kindersley Limited 9 Henrietta Street, London WC2E 8PS

Reprinted 1989, 1990

British Library Cataloguing in Publication Data
Shell
1. Molluscs. Shells - Field guides
I. Title II. Series
594'.0471

ISBN 0-86318-341-7

Colour reproduction by Colourscan, Singapore
Typeset by Windsor Graphics, Ringwood, Hampshire
Printed in Italy by A. Mondadori Editore, Verona

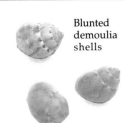

Blunted demoulia shells

Contents

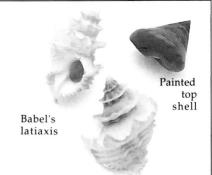

Babel's latiaxis

Painted top shell

What is a shell?

WHEN WE THINK OF A SHELL, we usually picture the pretty specimens that can be collected from the beach during a seaside stroll. In fact, shells can describe many other types of casing. The word "shell" actually means a hard outer casing that encloses and protects a variety of things, from fruit to baby birds, from snails to scurrying crabs. Shells, sometimes no more than a hardened skin, sometimes thick and heavy like some mollusc shells, are always a means of protection - against predators and mechanical damage, against extreme temperatures. Egg shells protect the unborn, nut shells enclose fruit and protect the seeds that give rise to new life. Even insects are usually protected by a hardened and segmented outer skin, but none have developed the heavily-thickened shells found in crabs and lobsters. In living creatures, like lobsters, a shell is called an exoskeleton, or external skeleton. One drawback of an exoskeleton is that it does not grow as the creature does, so the old shell must be shed and replaced by a new one big enough to accommodate its larger size.

Hairs on husk

White acorn of nut

Shell

Seed

WORM SHELLS
Even worms can make shells! This colony, (left) found at the bottom of an estuary, contains hundreds of hard, coiling tubes. Each one was once the home of a tiny marine worm.

HAIRY NUT
The fruit of the tropical coconut palm (right) can be bought in most parts of the world to eat. A thick, hard, hairy shell, or husk, encases the sweet, milky juices and white flesh. A soft skin covers the coconut when growing, which is usually removed before selling.

LUCKY BEANS
Highly-polished sea beans or "lucky" beans grow in pods, mainly along the banks of the Amazon river in South America. They burst and drop their beans into the river. When they are carried to the sea they become polished by the salt water, and are often used as lucky charms.

Ostrich shell

ARMOURED ARMADILLO
The armadillo is one of the last remaining types of a group of armour-plated animals that flourished on earth over 50 million years ago.

EGG SHELLS
Many creatures lay eggs in which their young can develop outside of the mother's body. The best-known are those laid by birds. Fertilized eggs hatch into fledglings, like the baby pheasant above.

Pheasant hatching

BIG BIRD
At twenty times the size of a chicken egg, the ostrich shell is one of the largest eggs ever produced by a bird.

SKULL OR SHELL?
Unlike a shell, skeletons are internal, and enclosed by skin and flesh. However, you can look on a skull as being a type of shell, as it encloses and protects some soft organs, largely the brain, while at the same time providing a framework to support flesh and skin tissue. Mammals, birds, and reptiles all have internal skeletons, each one giving a creature its special shape.

Badger skull

Pincer

Segmented body

SCORPION CASE
Like all insects, scorpions are invertebrate creatures with a hardened outer casing that protects them. Insects are the most abundant of all creatures, and have long been thought to be closely related to the crustaceans (p. 22). Like the crabs and lobsters, the segmented and armoured insects must shed their hardened casing in order to grow.

Sting

Four pairs of walking legs

Creatures with shells

O_F ALL THE MANY DIFFERENT TYPES OF ANIMALS, only a few have a hard outer casing, or shell, to protect the internal organs of their bodies. Animals such as the mammals, birds, reptiles, and fishes, have developed an internal skeleton for this purpose. Tortoises, turtles, and terrapins are the only vertebrate animals that have both an internal skeleton and an external shell. Most of the other shelled creatures are invertebrates, which means they have no backbones, and many are very simple animals that have remained virtually unchanged for millions of years. Not all shells are the same: seashells and snail shells are made from layers of calcium carbonate, crab shells are formed from a substance called "chitin", while tortoise-shell is made from plates of bone covered by keratin - a protein found in human fingernails.

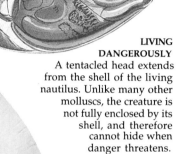

The nautilus

LIVING DANGEROUSLY
A tentacled head extends from the shell of the living nautilus. Unlike many other molluscs, the creature is not fully enclosed by its shell, and therefore cannot hide when danger threatens.

Molluscs

The largest group of shelled creatures are the molluscs, of which there are over 75,000 species, including snails, oysters, and octopuses. These versatile animals have evolved to live in the sea, in freshwater, and on land. Most molluscs have some kind of protective shell.

Edible land snail

Nautilus shell

SHELLED CEPHALOPOD
This shell belongs to the nautilus - a member of the most advanced group of molluscs: the cephalopods (p. 19)
The nautilus is the only kind of cephalopod that still has a true external shell.

EDIBLE SNAIL
One of the best-known shells is that of the edible land snail. These creatures are now quite rare in the wild but are commercially farmed to satisfy the gourmet's palate.

Portuguese oyster

INTERNAL SHELLS
Some molluscs have developed shells that are not visible from the outside. These spirula shells belong to a squid-like mollusc.

Spirula shells

SPINY SNAIL SHELL
Like the edible snail, this murex (spiny shell) belongs to a group of single-shelled molluscs known as "gastropods" (p. 12). This type of snail shell lives in the sea, where the variety of molluscs is greatest.

JEWEL IN THE SHELL
Pearls are formed inside oyster shells (see p. 36). These types of shell are known as bivalves - shells in two halves, that are joined by an elastic ligament and held together by strong muscles. Edible oysters are farmed commercially like edible land snails (above).

Venus comb murex

Reptiles

The reptiles are a varied group of cold-blooded vertebrate (with backbones) animals that includes snakes and lizards. Only the turtles, tortoises, and terrapins (p.28) have shells, and these are really only extensions of their own skeletons.

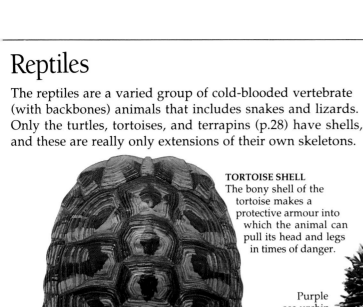

TORTOISE SHELL
The bony shell of the tortoise makes a protective armour into which the animal can pull its head and legs in times of danger.

Moorish tortoise and shell

SEA URCHIN TEST
The shell of a sea urchin is known as a "test", and is made up of closely fitting plates that enclose the creature's soft parts.

Tropical sea urchin

Purple sea urchin

A SPINY SKIN
The tests of living sea urchins are covered with hundreds of spines that help the creature to move around on the sea bed. Sometimes these spines are very sharp.

Echinoderms

This group of primitive sea-dwelling creatures includes starfish and sea cucumbers, which do not have shells, as well as sea urchins and sea potatoes (p. 20).

Florida sand dollar

SAND DOLLARS
These flattened sea urchins have very tiny spines and are adapted for life on sandy shores (see p. 21).

Crustaceans

There are over 30,000 types of crustaceans, including the lobsters, shrimps, crabs, and barnacles. Most crustaceans have some sort of jointed shell, or "carapace", and live in the oceans, although some have adapted to life in freshwater and on land.

Brown crab

BROWN HAIRY CRAB
This small crab lives in shallow-water rock pools, but relatives with leg spans of over 3.5 m (12 ft) can be found in deeper waters.

Atlantic barnacles

BARNACLES
Although they don't look much like the crabs or lobsters, barnacles are also crustaceans. All barnacles are marine creatures and spend their lives attached to a hard base such as another shell or the hull of a boat. Barnacle shells are strengthened by plates made from calcium.

EDIBLE CRAB
In many parts of the world crab meat is considered a delicacy, and crabs are fished in large numbers using baited pots. The main shell of the crab protects the internal organs, and the limbs are also covered in a hard, shell-like substance. This specimen has lost two of its eight legs.

Living in a whorl

DESPITE THE GREAT VARIETY in pattern, size, and weight, all seashells are made by the animals that live inside them, and all grow steadily "outwards". The whorl-shaped structures formed by the gastropod molluscs represent some of the most remarkable designs to be found anywhere in the natural world. Starting life as a minute larva, the mollusc sets about building its shell by depositing calcium from the mantle - a fleshy fold on the animal's body. As the creature grows, the shell is extended outwards in the form of a perfect spiral. Each type of seashell has a slightly different design, and this unique shape is passed on to each new generation.

ROCOCO DECORATION
The beautiful forms of seashells have influenced and inspired countless artists and architects throughout the centuries. Here, the radiating shape of a clam shell has been used to decorate an arched recess.

Buoyancy chambers

Cross-section of nautilus shell

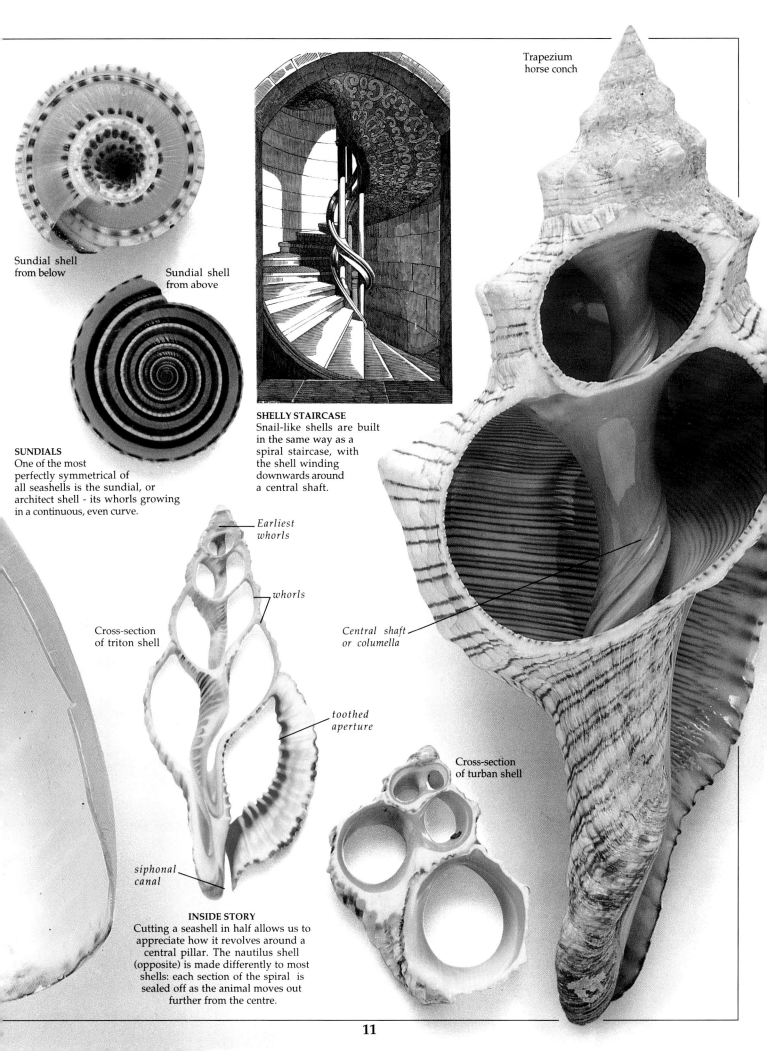

Sundial shell
from below

Sundial shell
from above

Trapezium
horse conch

SUNDIALS
One of the most
perfectly symmetrical of
all seashells is the sundial, or
architect shell - its whorls growing
in a continuous, even curve.

SHELLY STAIRCASE
Snail-like shells are built
in the same way as a
spiral staircase, with
the shell winding
downwards around
a central shaft.

Earliest
whorls

whorls

Cross-section
of triton shell

Central shaft
or columella

toothed
aperture

Cross-section
of turban shell

siphonal
canal

INSIDE STORY
Cutting a seashell in half allows us to
appreciate how it revolves around a
central pillar. The nautilus shell
(opposite) is made differently to most
shells: each section of the spiral is
sealed off as the animal moves out
further from the centre.

Snails of the world

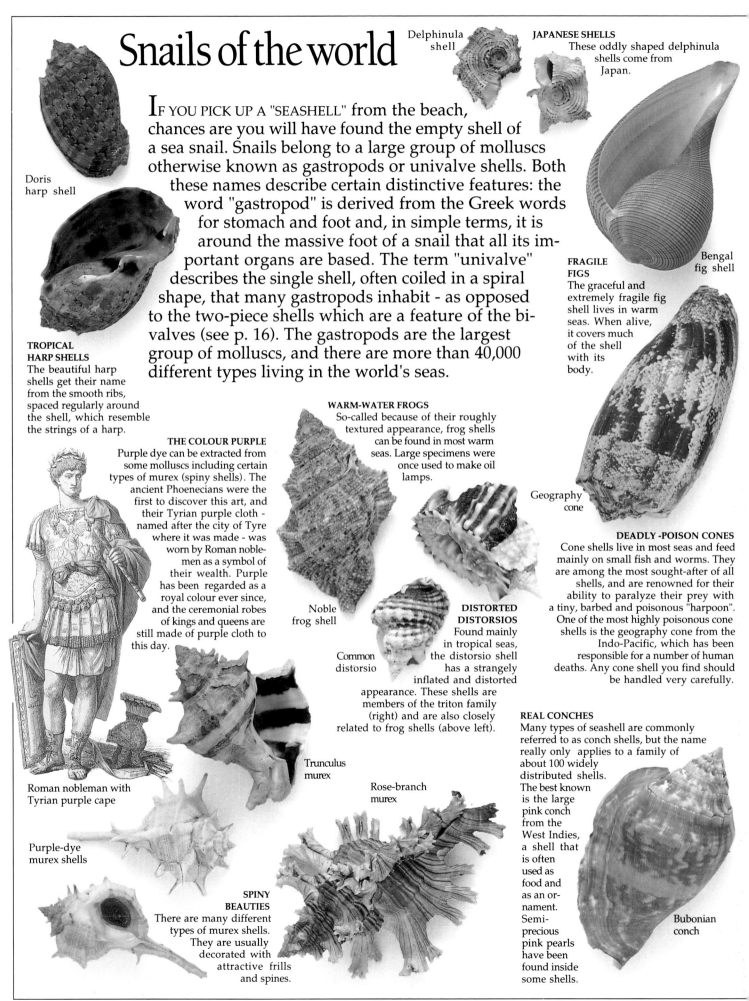

Delphinula shell

JAPANESE SHELLS
These oddly shaped delphinula shells come from Japan.

IF YOU PICK UP A "SEASHELL" from the beach, chances are you will have found the empty shell of a sea snail. Snails belong to a large group of molluscs otherwise known as gastropods or univalve shells. Both these names describe certain distinctive features: the word "gastropod" is derived from the Greek words for stomach and foot and, in simple terms, it is around the massive foot of a snail that all its important organs are based. The term "univalve" describes the single shell, often coiled in a spiral shape, that many gastropods inhabit - as opposed to the two-piece shells which are a feature of the bi-valves (see p. 16). The gastropods are the largest group of molluscs, and there are more than 40,000 different types living in the world's seas.

Doris harp shell

FRAGILE FIGS
The graceful and extremely fragile fig shell lives in warm seas. When alive, it covers much of the shell with its body.

Bengal fig shell

TROPICAL HARP SHELLS
The beautiful harp shells get their name from the smooth ribs, spaced regularly around the shell, which resemble the strings of a harp.

WARM-WATER FROGS
So-called because of their roughly textured appearance, frog shells can be found in most warm seas. Large specimens were once used to make oil lamps.

THE COLOUR PURPLE
Purple dye can be extracted from some molluscs including certain types of murex (spiny shells). The ancient Phoenecians were the first to discover this art, and their Tyrian purple cloth - named after the city of Tyre where it was made - was worn by Roman noble-men as a symbol of their wealth. Purple has been regarded as a royal colour ever since, and the ceremonial robes of kings and queens are still made of purple cloth to this day.

Geography cone

DEADLY-POISON CONES
Cone shells live in most seas and feed mainly on small fish and worms. They are among the most sought-after of all shells, and are renowned for their ability to paralyze their prey with a tiny, barbed and poisonous "harpoon". One of the most highly poisonous cone shells is the geography cone from the Indo-Pacific, which has been responsible for a number of human deaths. Any cone shell you find should be handled very carefully.

Noble frog shell

DISTORTED DISTORSIOS
Found mainly in tropical seas, the distorsio shell has a strangely inflated and distorted appearance. These shells are members of the triton family (right) and are also closely related to frog shells (above left).

Common distorsio

Roman nobleman with Tyrian purple cape

Trunculus murex

Rose-branch murex

REAL CONCHES
Many types of seashell are commonly referred to as conch shells, but the name really only applies to a family of about 100 widely distributed shells. The best known is the large pink conch from the West Indies, a shell that is often used as food and as an or-nament. Semi-precious pink pearls have been found inside some shells.

Purple-dye murex shells

SPINY BEAUTIES
There are many different types of murex shells. They are usually decorated with attractive frills and spines.

Bubonian conch

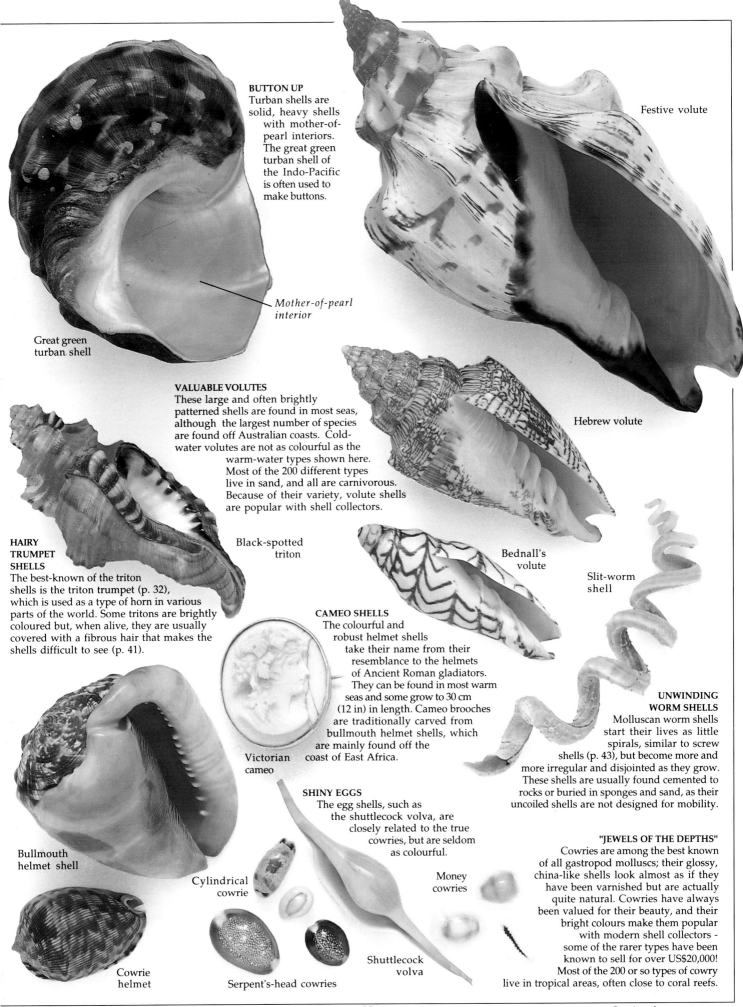

BUTTON UP
Turban shells are solid, heavy shells with mother-of-pearl interiors. The great green turban shell of the Indo-Pacific is often used to make buttons.

Festive volute

Mother-of-pearl interior

Great green turban shell

VALUABLE VOLUTES
These large and often brightly patterned shells are found in most seas, although the largest number of species are found off Australian coasts. Cold-water volutes are not as colourful as the warm-water types shown here. Most of the 200 different types live in sand, and all are carnivorous. Because of their variety, volute shells are popular with shell collectors.

Hebrew volute

HAIRY TRUMPET SHELLS
The best-known of the triton shells is the triton trumpet (p. 32), which is used as a type of horn in various parts of the world. Some tritons are brightly coloured but, when alive, they are usually covered with a fibrous hair that makes the shells difficult to see (p. 41).

Black-spotted triton

Bednall's volute

Slit-worm shell

CAMEO SHELLS
The colourful and robust helmet shells take their name from their resemblance to the helmets of Ancient Roman gladiators. They can be found in most warm seas and some grow to 30 cm (12 in) in length. Cameo brooches are traditionally carved from bullmouth helmet shells, which are mainly found off the coast of East Africa.

Victorian cameo

UNWINDING WORM SHELLS
Molluscan worm shells start their lives as little spirals, similar to screw shells (p. 43), but become more and more irregular and disjointed as they grow. These shells are usually found cemented to rocks or buried in sponges and sand, as their uncoiled shells are not designed for mobility.

SHINY EGGS
The egg shells, such as the shuttlecock volva, are closely related to the true cowries, but are seldom as colourful.

Bullmouth helmet shell

Cylindrical cowrie

Money cowries

"JEWELS OF THE DEPTHS"
Cowries are among the best known of all gastropod molluscs; their glossy, china-like shells look almost as if they have been varnished but are actually quite natural. Cowries have always been valued for their beauty, and their bright colours make them popular with modern shell collectors - some of the rarer types have been known to sell for over US$20,000! Most of the 200 or so types of cowry live in tropical areas, often close to coral reefs.

Cowrie helmet

Serpent's-head cowries

Shuttlecock volva

Continued on next page

Australian pheasant shell

Precious wentletrap

Green-lined paper bubble shell

White-banded bubble shell

STAIRCASE FORGERY
The wentletrap is one of the most distinctive of all seashells. Its name is derived from the German word *Wendeltrappe*, meaning "spiral staircase". This shell was once so rare that Chinese merchants are said to have sold forgeries made out of rice paste.

BREAKABLE BUBBLES
So called because of their fragile, inflated appearance, these paper-thin shells offer little protection to the mollusc, which is often much larger than the shell it carries.

European china limpets

LUSTROUS LIMPETS
Limpets are some of the best-known molluscs, being commonly found on coastal rocks, attached securely by their strong feet. Some types have a hole at the top of the shell, and are known as "keyhole limpets". The inside of a limpet shell often has an iridescent shine.

Humphrey's whelk

White-zoned goblet shell

Black-mouthed goblet shell

Pimpled dog whelk

Netted dog whelk

WHELKS OF THE WORLD
Found in great numbers in most of the world's seas - including both polar and tropical waters - the whelks are a very large family of marine molluscs, and in many parts of the world, are fished commercially.

Ridged goblet shell

Glans dog whelk

Clathrate dog whelk

GIANT PINK SEA -SNAIL
The mythical character Doctor Doolittle is famous for his ability to talk to animals of all kinds. In the film made about his adventures, the Doctor goes on a quest to find the fabulous giant pink sea-snail. Needless to say, no mollusc has ever been known to reach these proportions!

Freshwater snails

Although most types of snail live in the sea, many gastropods can also be found living in freshwater habitats. Some types absorb air from the water through gills, while others have lungs and have to come to the surface to breathe. The patterns and colours of freshwater shells tend to be fairly subdued compared to those of marine species. Freshwater snails can be found living on weeds and rushes or in mud and sand, but empty shells are often cast up on river banks, especially after flooding.

GIANT AFRICAN RIVER SNAIL
One of the largest freshwater snails occurs in the rivers of southeast Africa. Although it reaches a length of more than12 cm (5 in), the shell of the giant African river snail is amazingly lightweight and fragile. In the sea, a shell of this size would normally be covered with all sorts of encrusting growths, but, in freshwater, shells usually have a coat of algae that is easily removed.

OUT OF AFRICA
The strange-looking tiphorbia snail is just one of the hundreds of unique snail shells found in Lake Tanganyka in Africa. This huge expanse of landlocked water has developed a range of molluscs that are more like marine than freshwater gastropods.

GREAT POND SNAIL
This fragile snail is extremely common in lakes and ponds all over Europe. When alive, the shell has a greenish hue, although it is actually semi-transparent and it is the colour of the mollusc inside that can be seen.

RAM'S HORN SHELL
The flattened spiral shape of the ram's horn snail is fairly common.

Ram's horn shell

VIVIPARUS SNAIL
Owning one of the largest shells of European fresh-water snails, the banded viviparus snail gives birth to live young.

Giant African river snail

Land snails

In order to survive, land snails need to remain moist, so they are usually most active at night or when conditions are dull and wet. In dry conditions many types of snail can remain totally inactive for long periods, thereby retaining both energy and moisture. One museum specimen - thought to be long dead - was removed from a display case for cleaning, and began to move out of its shell after several years of "hibernation"!

COLOURFUL CUBAN COLLECTABLES
The brightly coloured Cuban land snail is now protected by law because overcollecting has threatened the species' future.

Cuban land snails

CHOOSY ESCARGOT
Snails will eat most types of vegetation but are not especially keen on most healthy green garden plants.

REGIONAL RARITY
This extremely rare tropidophora snail is only ever found on the island of Madagascar in the Indian Ocean.

operculum

teeth

UPSIDE-DOWN SNAIL
This unusual snail from the South American rain forest grows with its spiral facing earthwards.

MASSIVE PEST
The large achatina snails occur naturally in Africa, where they are eaten, but they are considered pests in other parts of the tropics where they have been introduced by man.

SNAILS IN TREES
These typically bright-green snails are only found on Manus Island in the Pacific, and are on the official list of endangered species.

Manus Island snails

growth scar

Achatina snail

LEFT-HANDED SNAIL
Shells that coil in an anti-clockwise direction are known as "sinistral" or "left-handed" shells - a feature that is relatively common among land snails.

Left-handed Saô Tomé snail

operculum

ELEPHANT SNAIL
This strange looking shell is found only in Malaya, and owes its name to being extremely heavy and robust .

European striped snails

Common garden snails

COMMONER IN THE GARDEN
Although abundant in gardens, snails do less harm than their cousins, the slugs.

BANDING TOGETHER
The common European striped snail has a very variable pattern. The colour and number of bands vary according to the kind of environment occupied by the snails (see p. 41).

Homes with hinges

B IVALVES ARE AMONG THE BEST KNOWN of all marine creatures. Like the gastropods, bivalves are molluscs, but their shells are divided into two parts, or valves, that completely enclose and protect the soft body of the mollusc inside. The valves are connected by a shelly ridge or teeth that form a hinge, and can be opened and closed by strong muscles and ligaments. Compared to the gastropods, bivalves do not lead very active lives - unable to extend far out of their shells to crawl, many live embedded in sand and mud (see p. 42), or remain hidden in rock crevices, while others attach themselves to a hard surface. Bivalves feed by opening their valves and filtering water through their gills to catch tiny creatures in the water around them. Bivalves can occur in vast numbers: some areas of the seafloor are known to contain as many as 8,000 living shells of one type in an area of one square metre (1.2 square yards).

THE BIRTH OF VENUS
This detail from the famous painting by Botticelli shows Venus being born from a scallop shell.

Royal cloak scallop

SCURRYING SCALLOPS
Scallops are among the best known bivalve molluscs. Some scallops have the unique skill of opening and closing their valves to swim away rapidly when disturbed.

Pacific thorny oyster

SPINY OYSTER SHELL
Spiny, or thorny, oysters are also known as chrysanthemum shells because of their likeness to the spiky-petalled flowers. Although not related to the true oyster, they are similar in that they remain attached to a solid base throughout their lives.

Ligament

BUTTERFLY WINGS
Shiny, colourful tellin shells are often washed ashore still in pairs, often resembling butterfly wings .

Flat tellin

Toothed donax

BEAN CLAMS
Generally tiny and wedge-shaped, these creatures live in large numbers on warm-water beaches. Being so abundant, they are often used as food, especially in soups.

Thin tellin

Noble pen shell

SHELLY BATHING-TUB
The huge tridacna shell houses an animal that can feed up to twenty people! Common in the Molucca islands, here, it is being used as a child's bathing-tub.

THE GIANT PEN SHELL
The pinna, or pen shell, spends its life in an upright position with its tapered end semi-embedded in soft bases, usually among weeds. The giant pen shell, which lives in the Mediterranean, is one of the largest bivalve molluscs, occasionally reaching a length of 60 cm (2 ft).

OPEN AND SHUT CASE
Although bivalves spend much of their lives with their valves slightly apart, they must be able to close the gap quickly and securely to protect themselves from predators. For this purpose, the two halves of a bivalve shell match perfectly and, when shut, the opening can be just as impenetrable as the rest of the shell.

Cocks-comb oyster

Spiny sand cockle

Fluted giant clam

Baby noble pen shell

MINIATURE MAN-EATER
There are many different types and sizes of clams, but the biggest of all shelled molluscs is the giant clam, whose valves can measure 1.2 m (3.9 ft) and weigh over 250 kg (1/4 ton). These huge shells have been put to many uses by man, including bathtubs and feeding troughs, and the shell is so strong that it can be made into axe-heads with which to fell trees. Living clams are said to have killed pearl divers by trapping their arms or legs between the two valves.

Byssal threads are secreted by some bivalves to anchor themselves to a hard base.

Byssus

Strange seashells

Most seashells are either gastropods (p. 10) or bivalves (p. 16), but there are a few other groups of shelled creatures that bear little obvious resemblance to either group. The smallest and least-known mollusc group is the gastroverms; rare creatures with small, limpet-shaped shells that can live 5,000 m (3 miles) below the surface of the sea. Better known are the chitons, sometimes referred to as "coat-of-mail shells" because the shells are made up of eight separate plates. Scaphopods, or tusk shells as they are commonly called, have shells that look like elephants' tusks. Like the chitons, tusk shells are primitive creatures that can be found in most of the world's seas, even in shallow water. The most advanced of all the molluscs are the cephalopods (from the Greek words for head and foot) - so called because of their distinctive tentacled heads. This class includes the octopus, squid, cuttlefish, and nautilus - mostly free-swimming creatures that have evolved without true shells.

PARTS OF A CHITON
The shell of a chiton consists of eight plates, or valves, which are attached to the back of the soft-bodied animal. These valves are joined and surrounded by a stretchy muscular band known as a girdle, allowing the animal to move over irregular surfaces. When a chiton is detached from its ground, it curls up to protect its soft body.

Individual valves of a chiton

Olive chitons

Girdle

HOLDING ON TIGHT
Chitons are found living on solid objects such as rocks and other shells. Like limpets, they hold on tightly to the surface when disturbed.

SIZEABLE VARIETY
There are over 600 types of chiton and, although they are all roughly the same shape, they can vary greatly in size, from 2 mm (0.1 in) to over 300 mm (12 in) long.

Shelly plates

Underside of a chiton shell

TUSK SHELLS
Tusk shells live with their heads buried in sand or mud. They feed on microscopic organisms that they catch and pass to their mouth with club-shaped tentacles.

Shell

Feeding tentacles

Foot

Mantle

Common tusk shells

Elephant tusk shell

Sensory and feeding tentacles

VALUABLE ASSETS
The ivory tusks of elephants have always been highly prized, but tusk shells, too, were valuable. Like the famed money cowries (p.13), once used as currency in Africa and the South Sea Islands, strings of tusk shells were used as money and jewellery by some North American Indian tribes.

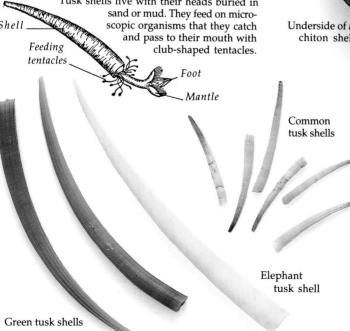

Green tusk shells

MYTHICAL SAILOR

It was once believed that the argonaut, or paper nautilus, "sailed" along using its shell as a boat and two of its arms as sails. However, this is not true; indeed, the wafer-thin "shell" is actually an egg-case used by the female argonaut and discarded after her eggs hatch.

Paper nautilus

Chambered nautilus shell

INTERNAL SHELL

Over millions of years the colourful cuttlefishes have discarded their external shells and evolved internal "cuttlebones" instead.

CHAMBERED NAUTILUS

The nautilus is the only cephalopod with a true external shell, but the animal only lives in the outer compartment. The inside of the shell is divided into many pearly chambers, which are filled with gas and help the nautilus to float. Buoyancy is controlled by taking in or letting out water.

Living common cuttlefish

SQUID

The squid's internal shell is a thin, transparent, pen-shaped tube that supports the animal's streamlined body. The squid propels itself backwards by jet propulsion, taking in and squirting out water, and can escape from danger by letting out a cloud of ink to hide its movements.

Long-finned squid

Spirula shells

Common spirula

SPIRAL SHELL

The coiled shell of the spirula has a chambered interior like that seen in the nautilus (see above), but this creature is more closely related to the cuttlefish, its shell being inside the animal's body.

GIANTS OF THE DEEP

Sailors' tales of enormous sea-monsters were probably based on sightings of huge cephalopods. The giant squid is the largest of all invertebrate animals, growing up to 20 m (67 ft) long.

Urchins of the sea

From below, the distinctive jaws of this living sea urchin are clearly visible.

THE SEA URCHINS belong to a large group of creatures called Echinoderms, a word derived from the Greek words for "spiny" and "skin". Various types of odd-looking creatures with strange-sounding names belong to this group, which includes the starfishes and the sea cucumbers, but the sea urchins, sea potatoes, sea biscuits, and sand dollars are the only ones with "shells". There are some 800 types of sea urchin living on the bottom of the world's oceans today. Although ancient in origins, they have adapted to most kinds of marine environment, from the polar regions to the tropics. They can be found in shallow or very deep water, and feed on both plants and animals. Echinoderms often show a five-rayed symmetry in their bodies, a feature that is particularly clear in starfish-type animals.

Pea urchins

The smallest urchins of Europe's seas, these pea urchins are commonly found in beachdrift.

Tropical sea urchin tests

SEA URCHIN TESTS
The shell of a sea urchin is known as a "test" and is made up of a series of plates that butt-up to each other or sometimes overlap. The test encloses and protects the soft parts of the animal. It is often shaped like a slightly flattened ball, and usually divided into five main areas. Sea urchin tests are often very colourful, and range in size from under 1 cm (0.5 in) to over 15 cm (6 in) in diameter.

SPIKY OR SPINELESS?
When alive, sea urchins are covered with numerous spines and tube "feet" that help the animal to move around. The spines are secured to the test by muscles around raised areas on the shell, which form a "ball-and-socket" joint that allows them to move in all directions. The spines on a sea urchin are used for locomotion, protection, and sometimes even as digging tools to burrow into rocks.

Sea urchin with all its spines

This edible sea urchin is the largest of Europe's urchins.

Sea urchin test exposed when spines removed

EATING URCHIN
Urchins feed with the aid of a complex, five-toothed jaw that resembles the part of an electric drill that grips the drill bit. The jaw is made up of bony plates operated by muscles, and is often referred to as "Arisotle's lantern" because of its similarity to certain types of old oil lamp. The mouth of a sea urchin is on the underside of the test, and always faces toward the sea bed.

"Aristotle's lantern", or jaw apparatus of sea urchin

Atlantic cidaris urchin

THE LONG AND THE SHORT OF IT
Cidaris sea urchins often have a lot of very tiny spines together with a few longer, thicker ones. This type lives in fairly deep water and can be found in the Atlantic Ocean and the Mediterranean.

SLATE-PENCIL SEA URCHIN
This type of sea urchin is commonly found on tropical coral reefs, where it tends to hide in crevices during the day, coming out to feed at night. The extremely long and heavy spines are sometimes used as wind chimes or as jewellery.

BURIED TREASURE?
The sand dollars are a distinctive group of sea urchins that have adapted specifically to life on sandy shores. Unlike other sea urchins, they have tiny spines and a flattened shape that improves their stability on the seabed and makes it easy for them to make shallow burrows in the sand. Sand dollars live in warm seas and are especially common in the Caribbean and Australian seas.

Indo-Pacific slate-pencil sea urchin

Sea potato with spines removed

Sea potato with spines

THE SEA POTATO
Like the sand dollar, the sea potato, or heart urchin, is adapted to live in sandy environments but often burrows deeply down to 20 cm (8 in) deep. The sea potato has modified, extra-long tube feet, which it can extend to pick up food from the surface of the sand.

Heart urchin in its burrow

Tube feet

Arrowhead sand dollar

Armour-plated animals

W HILE MANY CREATURES HAVE DEVELOPED strong outer casings that we call shells to protect their soft inner parts, one group has evolved what is more like a very hard and thick layer of skin. This large group is called the crustaceans, of which there are over 30,000 different types - including the lobsters, crabs, and crayfish - mostly living in the sea. Most of the crustaceans possess shells that are jointed - a bit like the suits of armour worn by medieval knights. Until recently, the crustaceans were thought to belong to the group known as the arthropods - the largest group of living creatures - which includes all the various types of insects. Nowadays, the crustaceans are considered by many experts to have evolved independently many millions of years ago, although there are many similarities between the two groups - including segmented bodies, jointed limbs, and the hardened outer skeleton, or shell, that is shed from time to time to allow the animal to grow.

THE LOBSTER IN ART
Besides inspiring the gourmet, lobsters have also inspired artists. This detail is from a 17th-century painting, "Still Life with Lobster", by Joris Van Son.

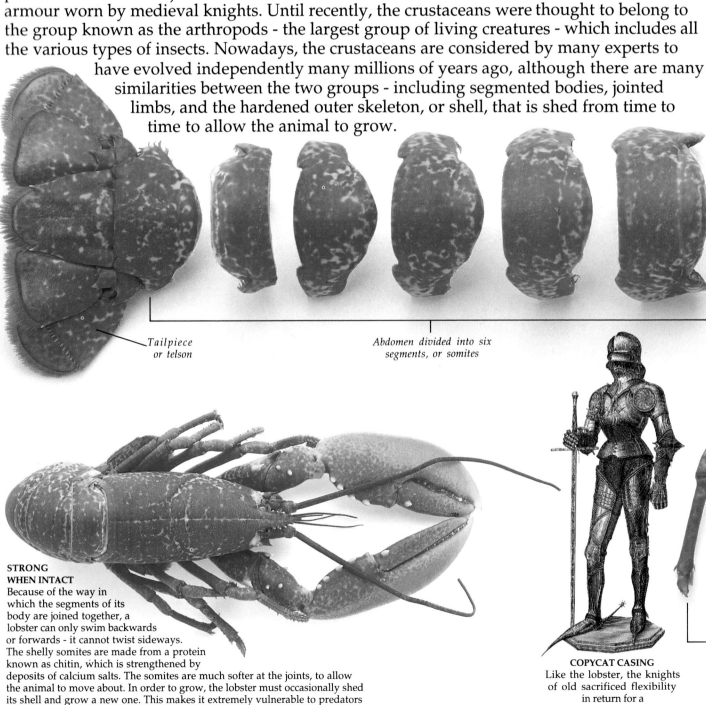

Tailpiece or telson

Abdomen divided into six segments, or somites

STRONG WHEN INTACT
Because of the way in which the segments of its body are joined together, a lobster can only swim backwards or forwards - it cannot twist sideways. The shelly somites are made from a protein known as chitin, which is strengthened by deposits of calcium salts. The somites are much softer at the joints, to allow the animal to move about. In order to grow, the lobster must occasionally shed its shell and grow a new one. This makes it extremely vulnerable to predators and the lobster wisely hides away until its new shell has had time to harden.

COPYCAT CASING
Like the lobster, the knights of old sacrificed flexibility in return for a protective suit of armour.

First leg, or cheliped

Carapace

Antennule

Eye

THE ARMOUR EXPLORED
Most crustaceans have a segmented, or
jointed, body at some time or other in
their lives: lobsters and shrimps
show this segmentation clearly as
adults. The bodies of these animals
are made up of a series of shelly,
overlapping rings with attached
appendages. In lobsters there are 19
such rings, or somites as they are
known. The tip of the head and the
tailpiece are not regarded as such,
since they do not have any true
appendages.

Antenna

Maxilliped

Moveable finger,
or claw

Ambulatory or walking legs

Fixed finger

Shells with ten legs

PERHAPS THE MOST familiar crustaceans are the crabs, lobsters, prawns, and crayfish. They all have the characteristic hardened, jointed shells, and ten legs, giving them the collective name of "decapods". But within the group crustacea, there is so much variety that it is impossible to find one feature common to every creature in the group that separates it from all other creatures. The members of the group range from tiny water fleas that live mainly in freshwater, to ostracods with their luminous bodies (p. 54); parasitic and limpet-like copepods, sometimes known as fish-lice, that attach themselves firmly to their hosts; and even the heavily armoured barnacles. Many of these creatures are microscopic and form a large part of "plankton", or the drifting life of the oceans. Plankton occurs in huge numbers in the world's oceans, and is an important part of the marine "food-chain", eaten by creatures that range in size from tiny molluscs to huge whales.

ALIVE AND SWIMMING
Crab larvae, like the common crab larva above, are free-swimming. Newly hatched at under 1mm (.039 in) long, the larva looks more like a mosquito than a crab.

Large claw is used to intimidate opponents

MEAN FIDDLER
Called the fiddler crab because the claws of the male look like a bow and fiddle, this crab lives in sandy burrows, or in sandy mud.

Pincer claws used for catching and holding prey as well as for defence

NO WAY OUT
Fishing for crabs and lobsters simply involves setting traps and waiting. The crab or lobster pots usually have two holes which reduce in size towards the centre of the basket. Crabs and lobsters, attracted by the bait within, crawl in and then are unable to get out, and have no choice but to await their fate.

19th-century engraving showing crab and lobster fishing scene on a beach

A NEW SUIT
Crabs, like all crustaceans, must shed their skins, or moult, in order to grow. At the time of moulting, cracks appear in a crab's shell, and the creature's soft parts begin to come through, gradually pushing aside the old shell. Crabs in the process of moulting are called "peelers" by fishermen, and when caught, are kept in tanks until they have moulted, so that they can be sold as "soft-shells" - a delicacy for the gourmet. Soft-shells usually eat their old shells, as the land crab on the right is demonstrating.

Pointed feet help crab to dig under sand

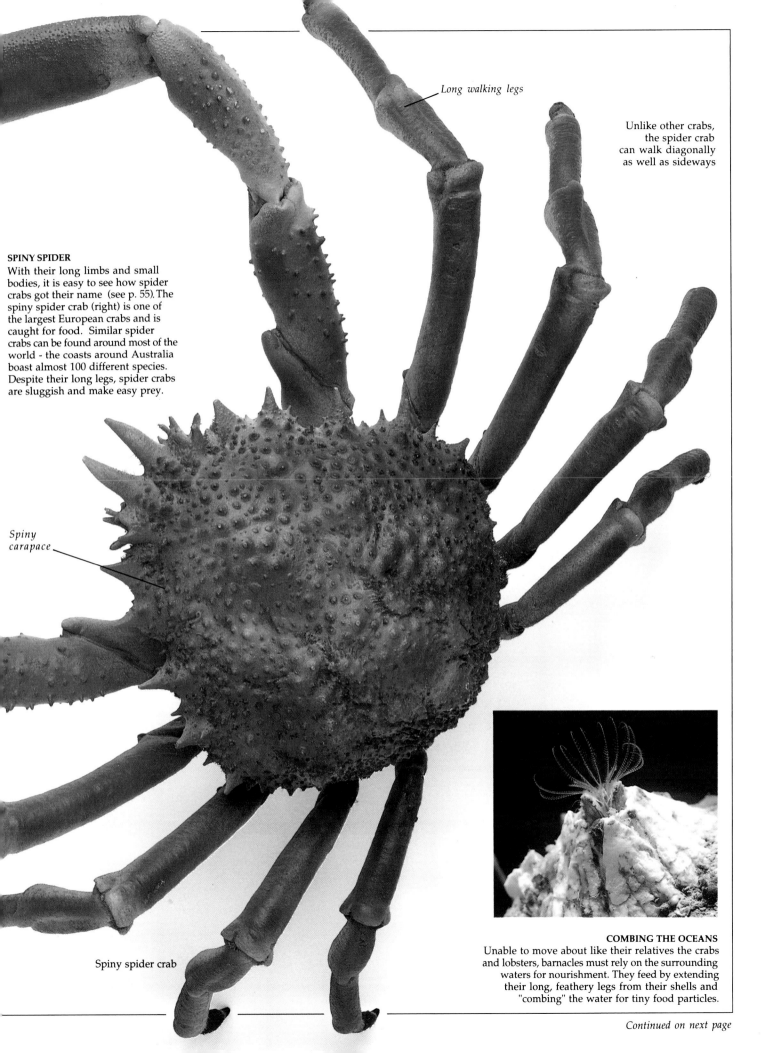

SPINY SPIDER
With their long limbs and small bodies, it is easy to see how spider crabs got their name (see p. 55). The spiny spider crab (right) is one of the largest European crabs and is caught for food. Similar spider crabs can be found around most of the world - the coasts around Australia boast almost 100 different species. Despite their long legs, spider crabs are sluggish and make easy prey.

Long walking legs

Unlike other crabs, the spider crab can walk diagonally as well as sideways

Spiny carapace

Spiny spider crab

COMBING THE OCEANS
Unable to move about like their relatives the crabs and lobsters, barnacles must rely on the surrounding waters for nourishment. They feed by extending their long, feathery legs from their shells and "combing" the water for tiny food particles.

Continued on next page

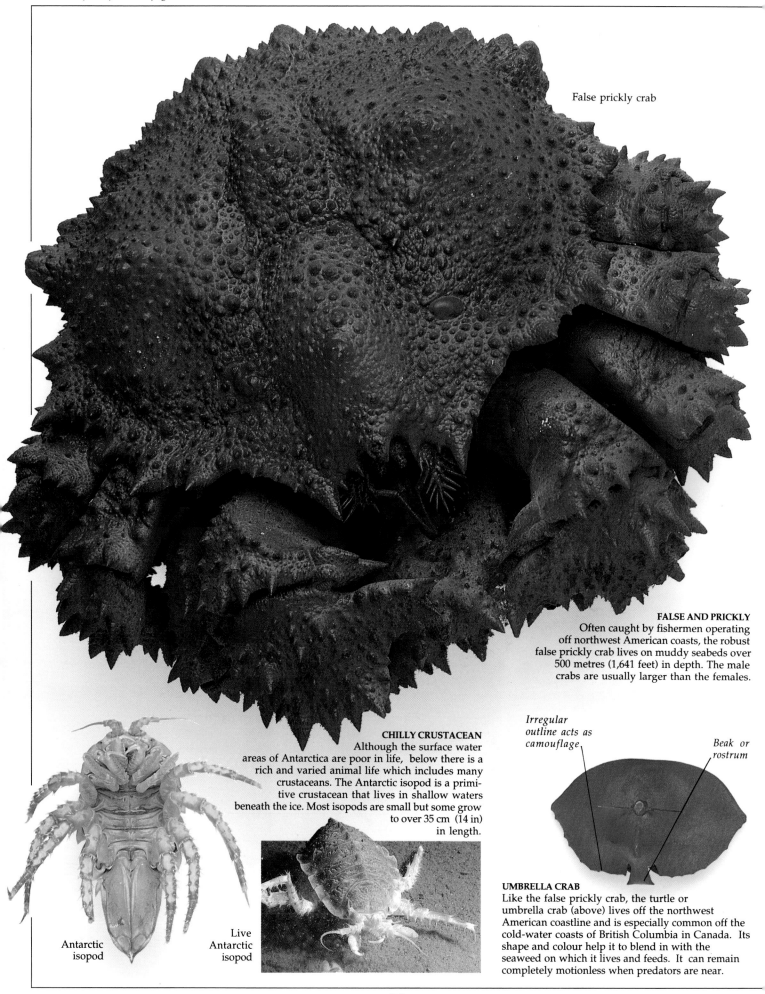

False prickly crab

FALSE AND PRICKLY
Often caught by fishermen operating off northwest American coasts, the robust false prickly crab lives on muddy seabeds over 500 metres (1,641 feet) in depth. The male crabs are usually larger than the females.

CHILLY CRUSTACEAN
Although the surface water areas of Antarctica are poor in life, below there is a rich and varied animal life which includes many crustaceans. The Antarctic isopod is a primitive crustacean that lives in shallow waters beneath the ice. Most isopods are small but some grow to over 35 cm (14 in) in length.

Antarctic isopod

Live Antarctic isopod

Irregular outline acts as camouflage

Beak or rostrum

UMBRELLA CRAB
Like the false prickly crab, the turtle or umbrella crab (above) lives off the northwest American coastline and is especially common off the cold-water coasts of British Columbia in Canada. Its shape and colour help it to blend in with the seaweed on which it lives and feeds. It can remain completely motionless when predators are near.

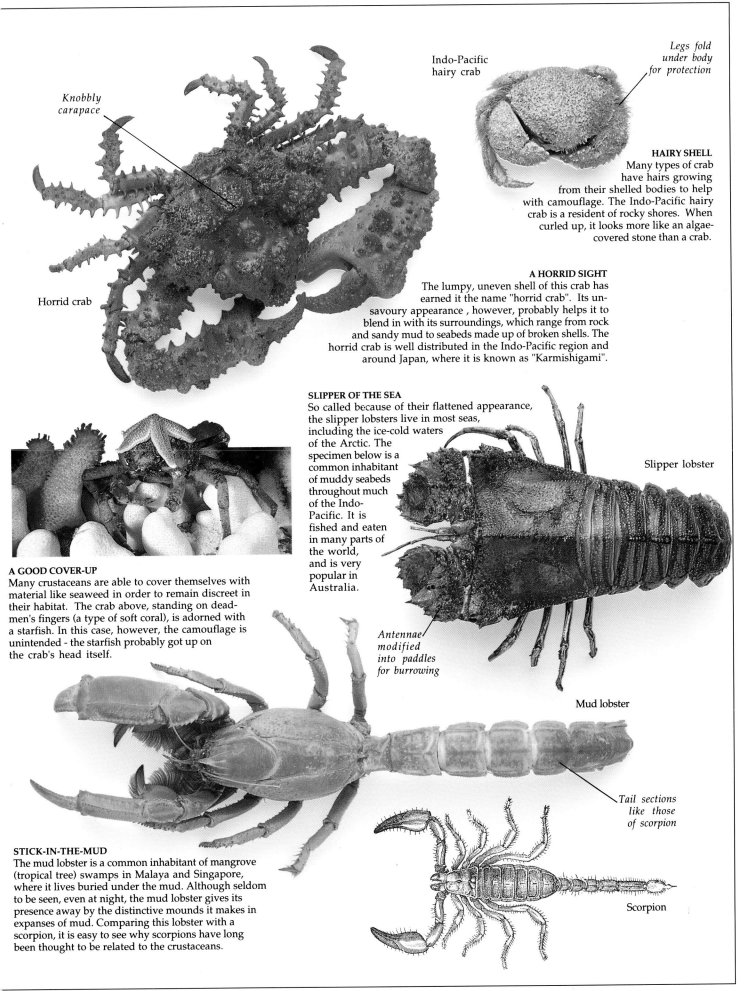

Knobbly carapace

Indo-Pacific hairy crab

Legs fold under body for protection

Horrid crab

HAIRY SHELL
Many types of crab have hairs growing from their shelled bodies to help with camouflage. The Indo-Pacific hairy crab is a resident of rocky shores. When curled up, it looks more like an algae-covered stone than a crab.

A HORRID SIGHT
The lumpy, uneven shell of this crab has earned it the name "horrid crab". Its un-savoury appearance , however, probably helps it to blend in with its surroundings, which range from rock and sandy mud to seabeds made up of broken shells. The horrid crab is well distributed in the Indo-Pacific region and around Japan, where it is known as "Karmishigami".

SLIPPER OF THE SEA
So called because of their flattened appearance, the slipper lobsters live in most seas, including the ice-cold waters of the Arctic. The specimen below is a common inhabitant of muddy seabeds throughout much of the Indo-Pacific. It is fished and eaten in many parts of the world, and is very popular in Australia.

Slipper lobster

A GOOD COVER-UP
Many crustaceans are able to cover themselves with material like seaweed in order to remain discreet in their habitat. The crab above, standing on dead-men's fingers (a type of soft coral), is adorned with a starfish. In this case, however, the camouflage is unintended - the starfish probably got up on the crab's head itself.

Antennae modified into paddles for burrowing

Mud lobster

Tail sections like those of scorpion

STICK-IN-THE-MUD
The mud lobster is a common inhabitant of mangrove (tropical tree) swamps in Malaya and Singapore, where it lives buried under the mud. Although seldom to be seen, even at night, the mud lobster gives its presence away by the distinctive mounds it makes in expanses of mud. Comparing this lobster with a scorpion, it is easy to see why scorpions have long been thought to be related to the crustaceans.

Scorpion

Turtles, tortoises, and terrapins

TORTOISES, TURTLES, AND TERRAPINS are an ancient and closely related family, having lived on this planet since the age of the dinosaurs. Being reptiles, they are vertebrates like us, but are unique in the animal kingdom in that they have a solid outer shell as well as an internal skeleton. They are also "cold-blooded" creatures because they are unable to regulate their body temperatures internally. They can, however, raise their body temperature by basking in the sun. Most tortoises in the wild tend to live in the warmer parts of the world. Tortoises can be found in colder areas, too, but they then need to hibernate during the winter months. Although they seem very similar, tortoises, turtles, and terrapins have evolved to suit different environments: tortoises usually live on land, terrapins in freshwater, and all turtles but one live in the sea.

THE HARE AND THE TORTOISE
Tortoises are famous for their slow movements, but as the well-known fable "The Hare and the Tortoise" tells us, perseverance is more important than speed. Despite its slowness, the tortoise has managed to survive on earth with very little change for over 250 million years, relying mainly on its hard shell for protection.

Stinkpot turtle

Red-eared slider

Painted turtle

BASKING TERRAPINS
Terrapins live in freshwater habitats and can often be seen basking in the sun on rocks or river-banks. Usually smaller than either tortoises or turtles, these endearing little creatures are often kept as pets in freshwater tanks.

Clawed foot

Scutes, or scales, cover bony carapace

On the Galapagos Islands in the Pacific live "giant" tortoises that can reach one-and-a-half metres (4.92 ft) in length.

Plastron

TORTOISE TALE
The armour-plated tortoise has a distinctive domed shell, or carapace, on top and a flat, bony plate, called a plastron, below. This shell protects most of the animal's soft tissues, and its exposed legs and head can be drawn quickly inside the shell when danger threatens. The tortoise does not have teeth but can still inflict a painful bite with the aid of its strong jaws and the sharp, horny tissue that surrounds them, like the beak of a bird.

TORTOISE EXPOSED

From below, once the animal and the plastron or "under-shell" have been removed, you can see clearly how the carapace of a chelonian (the group name for all turtles, tortoises, and terrapins) is really just an extension of its ribcage. Because its ribs are fused with its shell, the tortoise is unable to expand its lungs and must rely on the movements of its head and limbs to pump in fresh air. Although very similar to its cousin the turtle, the latter has a less domed, more streamlined shell, and has webbed feet for fast swimming.

A LEATHER SHELL?
The largest of all living turtles, this giant has a leathery, ridged skin above and below its body, instead of the usual horny plates, hence the name "leatherback". It tends to live in the middle of the sea, rather than the bottom.

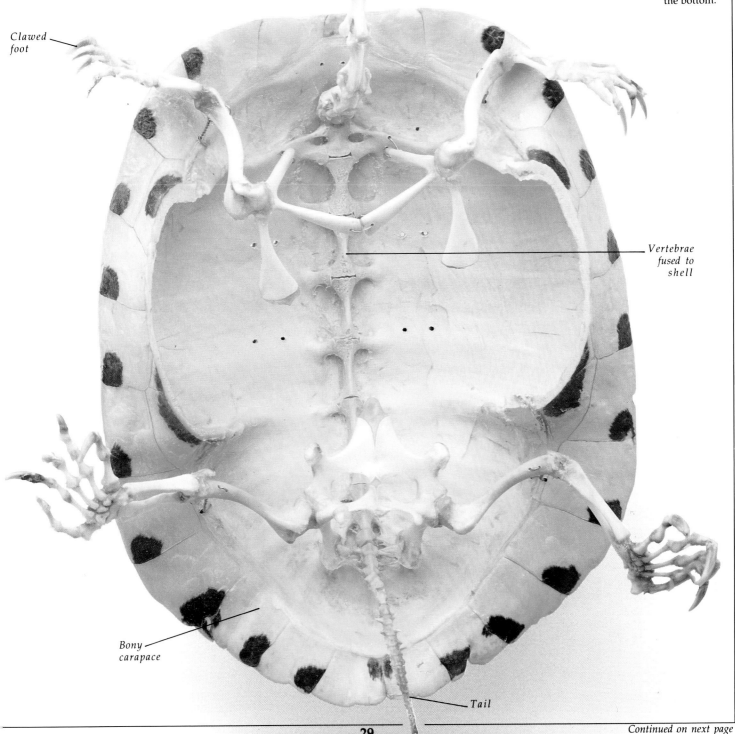

Skull

Neck vertebra

Clawed foot

Vertebrae fused to shell

Bony carapace

Tail

Continued on next page

Tortoiseshell designs

There are over 200 different types of tortoise, turtle, and terrapin, all belonging to a reptilian group called the Chelonia. Although the structure of the shell is essentially the same in most of the creatures in this group, the markings on the bony scales that make up the carapace are often very distinctive and provide a useful means of identification. As with most living creatures, young specimens have different coloration from those found in adults.

MOCK TURTLE
In Lewis Carroll's story, "Alice's Adventures in Wonderland", Alice encounters many strange creatures on her travels, one of which is the melancholy Mock Turtle. Encouraged by the Gryphon, the Mock Turtle teaches Alice how to dance the famous "Lobster Quadrille", and tearfully laments the fact that he is not a true turtle. This leads him to sing "Turtle Soup", a sad reminder that his days are numbered.

Young leopard tortoise carapace

Juvenile leopard tortoise carapace

LEOPARD BY NAME, TORTOISE BY NATURE
The leopard tortoise gets its name from the speckled markings on its domed shell. The young shells (above and left) have not yet developed the distinctive pattern visible on the adult (far left). Although widely distributed on the African continent, the leopard tortoise prefers savannah and woodland areas, where it feeds on a variety of plants.

AN EXTRA WEIGHT
As if the weight of its own enormous shell were not enough to carry, this giant tortoise is also bearing the load of Lord Rothschild, the world-famous 19th-century naturalist. Giant tortoises were first discovered by Charles Darwin on his voyage to the Galapagos Islands, and they have fascinated naturalists ever since. Lord Rothschild was especially keen on these slow-moving creatures, and kept many at his museum in Tring, England.

Main carapace colour is yellow

Mature leopard tortoise carapace

During the late 19th and early 20th
century, it was fashionable to
have objects sculpted from
tortoiseshell. The most beautiful
tortoiseshell comes from the
hawksbill turtle.

Victorian tortoiseshell
haircomb

1920s tortoise-
shell box

Victorian "lorgnette" glasses
made from tortoiseshell

GLIDING WITH EASE
Hawksbill turtles are extremely fast
swimmers, their long, paddle-like
flippers and low shells helping them
to glide smoothly through the water.
Marine turtles come ashore to
lay their eggs and, on
land, they are even
slower than
tortoises.

*Thick
overlapping
plates*

Natural
hawksbill
tortoiseshell

Hawksbill turtles

One of the best-known of all marine
turtles is the hawksbill. Once hunted for
its beautiful shell (above), this turtle is now
on the official list of endangered species and
imports are banned in many countries. It can be
found in most warm seas around the world and
feeds on molluscs and crustaceans.

A growing shell

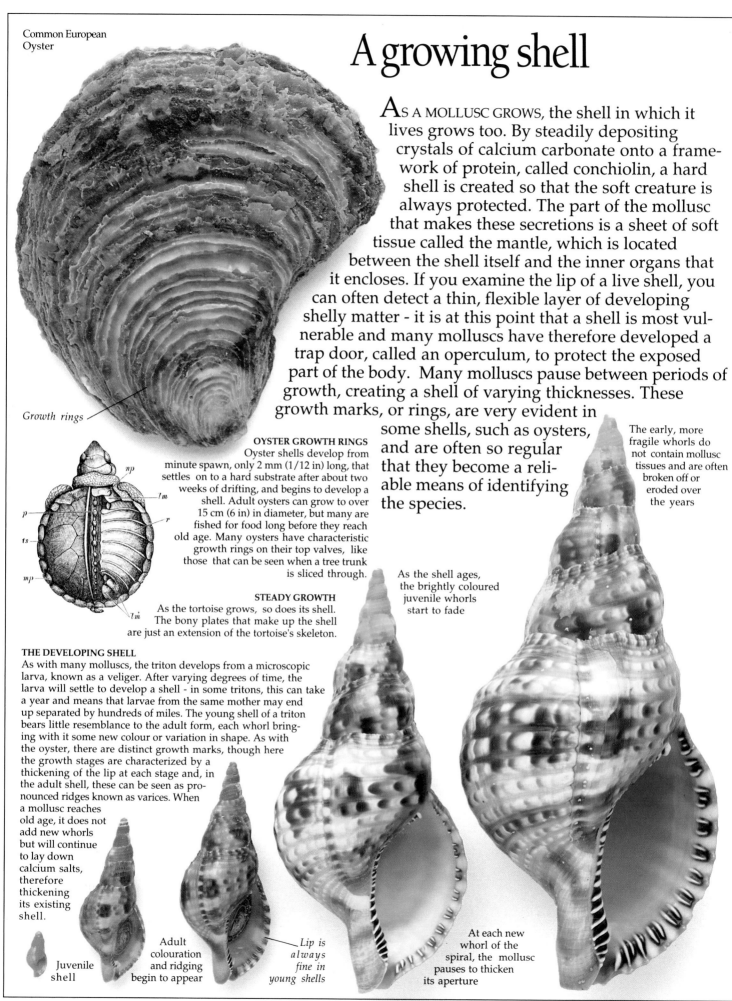

Common European Oyster

Growth rings

As A MOLLUSC GROWS, the shell in which it lives grows too. By steadily depositing crystals of calcium carbonate onto a framework of protein, called conchiolin, a hard shell is created so that the soft creature is always protected. The part of the mollusc that makes these secretions is a sheet of soft tissue called the mantle, which is located between the shell itself and the inner organs that it encloses. If you examine the lip of a live shell, you can often detect a thin, flexible layer of developing shelly matter - it is at this point that a shell is most vulnerable and many molluscs have therefore developed a trap door, called an operculum, to protect the exposed part of the body. Many molluscs pause between periods of growth, creating a shell of varying thicknesses. These growth marks, or rings, are very evident in some shells, such as oysters, and are often so regular that they become a reliable means of identifying the species.

OYSTER GROWTH RINGS
Oyster shells develop from minute spawn, only 2 mm (1/12 in) long, that settles on to a hard substrate after about two weeks of drifting, and begins to develop a shell. Adult oysters can grow to over 15 cm (6 in) in diameter, but many are fished for food long before they reach old age. Many oysters have characteristic growth rings on their top valves, like those that can be seen when a tree trunk is sliced through.

STEADY GROWTH
As the tortoise grows, so does its shell. The bony plates that make up the shell are just an extension of the tortoise's skeleton.

THE DEVELOPING SHELL
As with many molluscs, the triton develops from a microscopic larva, known as a veliger. After varying degrees of time, the larva will settle to develop a shell - in some tritons, this can take a year and means that larvae from the same mother may end up separated by hundreds of miles. The young shell of a triton bears little resemblance to the adult form, each whorl bringing with it some new colour or variation in shape. As with the oyster, there are distinct growth marks, though here the growth stages are characterized by a thickening of the lip at each stage and, in the adult shell, these can be seen as pronounced ridges known as varices. When a mollusc reaches old age, it does not add new whorls but will continue to lay down calcium salts, therefore thickening its existing shell.

The early, more fragile whorls do not contain mollusc tissues and are often broken off or eroded over the years

As the shell ages, the brightly coloured juvenile whorls start to fade

Juvenile shell

Adult colouration and ridging begin to appear

Lip is always fine in young shells

At each new whorl of the spiral, the mollusc pauses to thicken its aperture

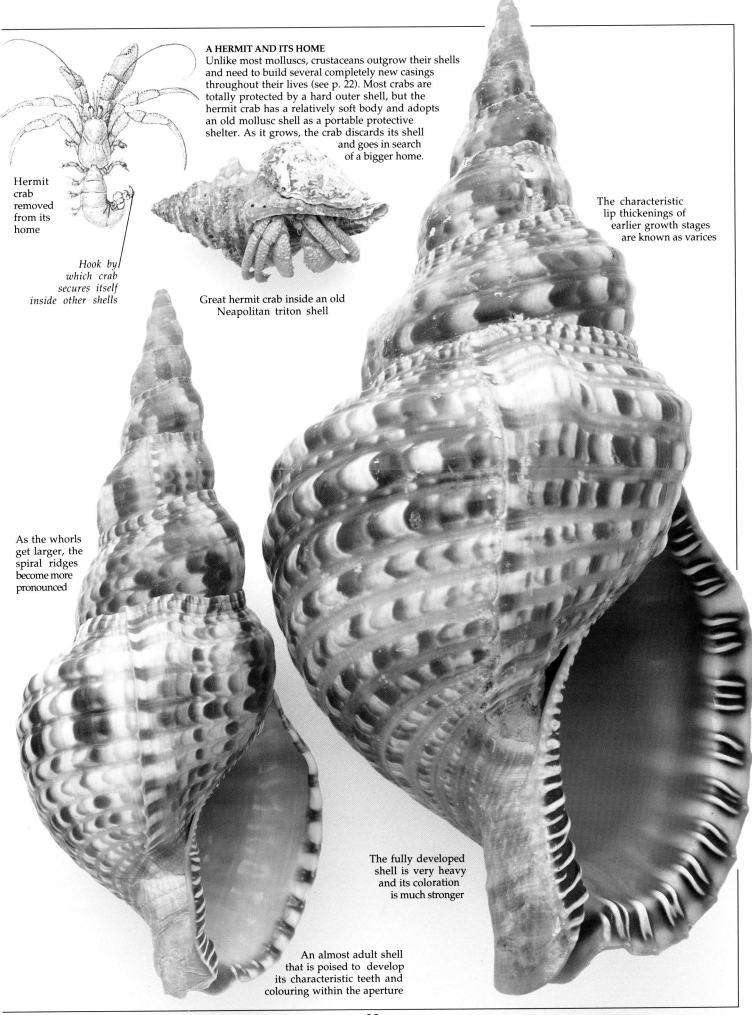

A HERMIT AND ITS HOME
Unlike most molluscs, crustaceans outgrow their shells and need to build several completely new casings throughout their lives (see p. 22). Most crabs are totally protected by a hard outer shell, but the hermit crab has a relatively soft body and adopts an old mollusc shell as a portable protective shelter. As it grows, the crab discards its shell and goes in search of a bigger home.

Hermit crab removed from its home

Hook by which crab secures itself inside other shells

Great hermit crab inside an old Neapolitan triton shell

The characteristic lip thickenings of earlier growth stages are known as varices

As the whorls get larger, the spiral ridges become more pronounced

The fully developed shell is very heavy and its coloration is much stronger

An almost adult shell that is poised to develop its characteristic teeth and colouring within the aperture

Shells for gourmets

As a food resource, the sea offers an incredibly varied menu. Apart from ordinary fish, lobsters, and crabs, sea urchins and most molluscs are eaten all around the world. Many people who live near the sea survive almost entirely on seafood, and it is true that these are often the healthiest people - most seafood being rich in protein but low in calories. It is rather strange that many people shy away from accepting the French delicacy of snails, but are quite happy to eat squid or a plate of spaghetti marinara, filled with small clams. Bivalve shells are the most popular form of shellfish; varieties of oyster, clam, scallop, cockle, and mussel are found in many parts of the world, and several types are farmed solely for human consumption. Some gastropods are also very popular; the abalone is sometimes eaten as steaks in parts of North America, Japan, and Australia, as is the Queen conch throughout the Caribbean. In Europe, the whelk, or "buckie", is often fished commercially. For the shell collector, the fish market is often the best source for finding local shells, especially in tropical areas.

THE WALRUS AND THE CARPENTER
In the Lewis Carroll story "Alice's Adventures Through the Looking Glass", the walrus and the carpenter ask some young oysters to take a stroll along the beach, and then proceed to eat them with bread and butter!

Hinge
ligament

THE POPULAR CLAM
Often used in soups and sauces, this small but abundant clam is found in great quantities in the seas of northern Europe. Its American cousin, a much larger but otherwise very similar shell called the Atlantic surf clam, is a major food source; some 20 million kg (45 million lbs) of its meat are fished each year between Nova Scotia and North Carolina.

OYSTER CATCHER
With its long, sharp beak, the oyster catcher is well equipped for digging bivalves from the sand.

"ALIVE, ALIVE O"
Among the most popular of all edible molluscs is the oyster - each ocean has its own varieties, some more than double the size of these live Portuguese oysters. The traditional method of eating oysters is to swallow them whole, straight from the shell, uncooked and complete with all the natural juices. In times past, it was not uncommon to see street vendors serving live oysters to be eaten on the spot.

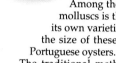

Mantle
tissue

Adductor
muscle
tissue

Fresh oysters being sold
in a street market

Portuguese
Oysters

Common
cockle

Hinge

*Exhalant
siphon*

Foot

*Inhalant
siphon*

Gills

HEART
OF A COCKLE
The small body of the common cockle
is made up of all the same parts as
the larger shellfish. Like most other seafood,
cockles are best eaten fresh, but can also be found
pickled in jars. The pickling process
preserves the meat and
keeps it from spoiling.

MOUTHWATERING MUSSELS
Easily found in fish markets and very tasty, mussels
can be cooked and served with the open shell in a
variety of sauces or used in soups - the most
popular dish is probably the French *moules
marinières*. In Europe and
America, the most
common mussels are
normally blue, but
the green New
Zealand variety
shown here is
exported
world-
wide.

New Zealand
mussel

*Byssus or byssal
threads anchor
shell to solid
ground*

*Adductor
muscle*

*Hinge
ligament*

BREAKING
AND ENTERING
Molluscs are an important source
of food for many creatures other
than humans. The Californian
sea otter tugs abalones and
other molluscs from their
underwater homes and
uses a rock to smash
open the shells as he
lies on his back in the water.

A NATURAL DISH
The distinctively shaped shell of a
scallop makes a natural dish on which
to serve scallop meat. One of the most
commonly eaten varieties has one flat valve
and one concave, or dish-shaped, valve.
In Europe, the whole of the mollusc
is usually eaten, whereas
in America only
the white
muscle is
used.

*White muscle
tissue*

Concave
lower valve

Bottom valve
containing
mollusc

A pearl is born

ALTHOUGH THEY ARE HIGHLY PRIZED by humans, pearls begin their lives as a nuisance to the creatures that make them. If a foreign body - such as a tiny piece of rock or the egg of a parasite - becomes lodged between the mantle of a mollusc and its shell, the animal will cover the object with layers of shelly material, or nacre, so creating a pearl. In the case of pearl oyster shells, which have an iridescent interior, the pearls that are formed are as beautiful and lustrous as the inside of the shell. All types of molluscs are capable of producing pearls, although bivalves are more likely to do so because they tend to live in a fixed position and are unable to extend out of their shells to dislodge a foreign body. Naturally formed pearls are extremely rare, but a way of cultivating pearls artificially was perfected by the Japanese at the start of this century, making cheaper pearls more accessible. By inserting an artificial nucleus into a living oyster, a good-sized "cultured" pearl is virtually guaranteed after between three and five years. The pearl industry is now so large that around 500 million pearls are produced each year.

PEARLY BUDDHAS
Although the Japanese are credited with perfecting the process of pearl cultivation, the Chinese had discovered pearlification and put it to use - over 700 years before. Little clay figures of the god Buddha were inserted inside freshwater mussels and left for about a year, after which the shells would be opened to reveal perfectly coated mother-of-pearl figurines. Some mussels have been preserved with the tiny Buddhas still in place, but they were originally intended to be used as jewellery charms.

BLISTERING BIVALVES
A dome-shaped pearl that has developed while attached to the inside surface of an oyster shell is known as a blister pearl. These are quite common and are of little commercial value, being generally used for purely decorative purposes. Very often the blisters reveal the nature of the object which is embedded against the shell, which may be a tiny crab or fish.

Freshwater pearls

PEARL OYSTER
Even small oysters can produce reasonably large pearls, although the older and larger the shell, the greater the chance of finding a good-sized pearl. This type of oyster grows to about 20 cm (8 in), and is common throughout the Indo-Pacific as well as the eastern Mediterranean, which it penetrated recently via the Suez Canal.

QUEEN MARY'S PEARLS
Before the advent of cultured pearls, jewellery made with natural pearls was extremely expensive and therefore a symbol of great wealth or status. Queen Mary of England is remembered for the long strings of pearls she wore.

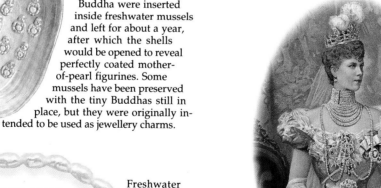

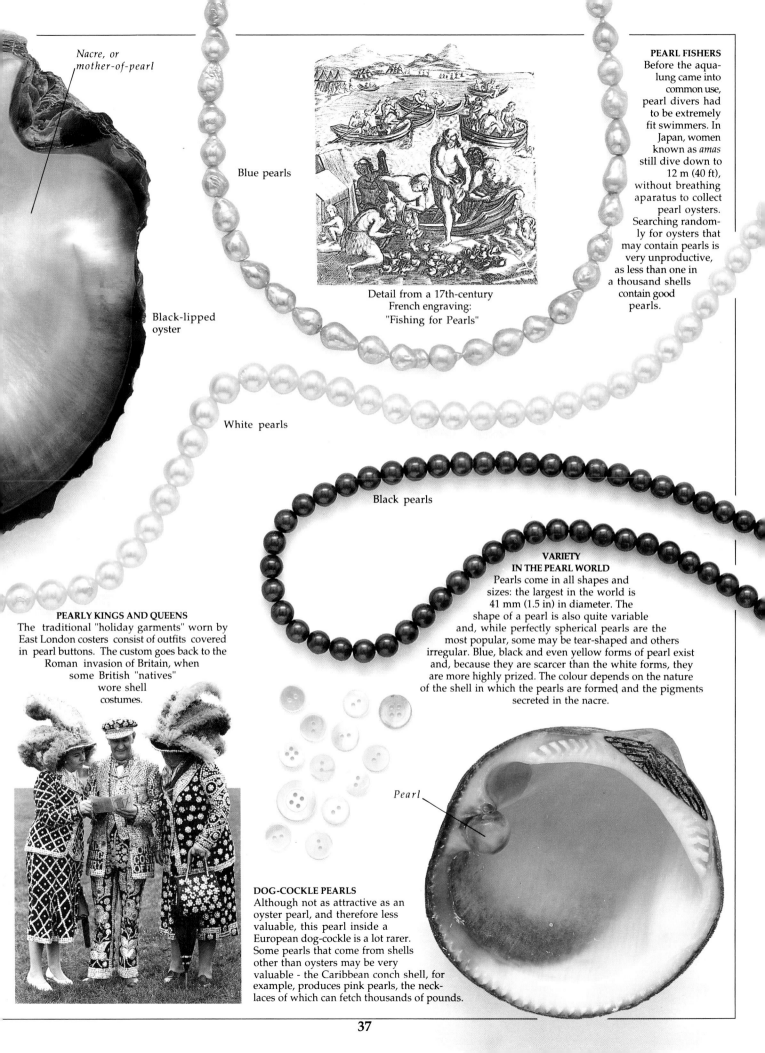

Nacre, or mother-of-pearl

Blue pearls

Black-lipped oyster

White pearls

Black pearls

Detail from a 17th-century French engraving: "Fishing for Pearls"

PEARL FISHERS

Before the aqua-lung came into common use, pearl divers had to be extremely fit swimmers. In Japan, women known as *amas* still dive down to 12 m (40 ft), without breathing aparatus to collect pearl oysters. Searching random-ly for oysters that may contain pearls is very unproductive, as less than one in a thousand shells contain good pearls.

VARIETY IN THE PEARL WORLD

Pearls come in all shapes and sizes: the largest in the world is 41 mm (1.5 in) in diameter. The shape of a pearl is also quite variable and, while perfectly spherical pearls are the most popular, some may be tear-shaped and others irregular. Blue, black and even yellow forms of pearl exist and, because they are scarcer than the white forms, they are more highly prized. The colour depends on the nature of the shell in which the pearls are formed and the pigments secreted in the nacre.

Pearl

PEARLY KINGS AND QUEENS

The traditional "holiday garments" worn by East London costers consist of outfits covered in pearl buttons. The custom goes back to the Roman invasion of Britain, when some British "natives" wore shell costumes.

DOG-COCKLE PEARLS

Although not as attractive as an oyster pearl, and therefore less valuable, this pearl inside a European dog-cockle is a lot rarer. Some pearls that come from shells other than oysters may be very valuable - the Caribbean conch shell, for example, produces pink pearls, the neck-laces of which can fetch thousands of pounds.

Fossil finds

WE ARE LUCKY IN THAT it is quite easy to trace the history of shelled animals back through many millions of years. Although the soft parts of an animal will rot away quickly after it dies, the shells are easily preserved for long periods of time and can often be found as fossils (remains of the empty shell that have been turned into rock over millions of years, or identical casts of the long-gone shell). Fossil evidence shows how certain species have changed with the passage of time; in many cases animals have had to evolve in order to cope with changes in their environment, such as a change in temperature or in the sources of food available. Some animals have remained unchanged, presumably because they are in a stable niche and in perfect harmony with their environment.

Fossilized sand dollar from Florida, U.S.A.

tentacled head would have emerged from here.

Fossilized ammonites from Dorset, England

Curled-up fossil trilobites

"Snakestone" ammonite forgery

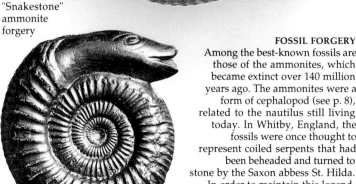

FOSSIL FORGERY
Among the best-known fossils are those of the ammonites, which became extinct over 140 million years ago. The ammonites were a form of cephalopod (see p. 8), related to the nautilus still living today. In Whitby, England, the fossils were once thought to represent coiled serpents that had been beheaded and turned to stone by the Saxon abbess St. Hilda. In order to maintain this legend, snakes' heads were commonly carved on fossil ammonites sold to tourists in the area.

Uncurled trilobite

TALE OF THE TRILOBITES
The trilobites were another common animal that became extinct some 248 million years ago. These were primitive marine creatures related to the crustaceans that abound in our seas today. Like lobsters and crabs, trilobites had the ability to shed their armour-plated skin, so trilobite fossils are fairly common. Some are found curled-up, like a modern woodlouse, for protection. There are known to have been thousands of species of trilobite - the largest type measuring some 70 cm (28 in) long.

Impression of trilobite embedded in rock

Fossil lampshells embedded in rock

Fossilized lampshells

LAMPSHELLS
Belonging in a class all their own, the creatures known as brachiopods, or lampshells, were once extremely common. Their name comes from their resemblance to certain types of ancient oil lamps. Lampshells resemble bivalve molluscs but are unrelated. Fossil records go back almost 600 million years, and fossil lampshells are sometimes found in large numbers.

Modern brachiopod

Recent Neapolitan triton shell

Fossilized Neapolitan triton shell

ALIVE AND WELL AFTER 3 MILLION YEARS
A creature that has been in tune with its environment for a long time, the Neapolitan triton has hardly changed at all for 3 million years. Although this is not very long in geological terms, many similar types have died out, implying that the Neapolitan triton has truly found the secret to success.

BLOWING THE TRUMPET
Man has inhabited the earth for a very short time compared to creatures with shells, but we have used the empty shells in various ways for thousands of years. Horns made from conch and triton shells have been used to signal over large distances by civilizations in all parts of the world.

Horseshoe crab from beneath

Tail spine

Horseshoe-shaped carapace (shell)

Horseshoe crab

PRESERVATION OF FOSSILS
The condition of a fossil is dependent mainly on its age and the type of sediment in which it was deposited. Many fossils are solidly embedded in hard rock while others exist in softer substances such as clay. The fossil shells shown here were deposited only a couple of million years ago, and were found in soft earth on a cliff only a little way from the sea. They are beautifully preserved, and as delicate as modern ones.

LIVING FOSSIL
The horseshoe crab, or king crab - commonly found living in the seas off northeast America - is a "living fossil", having remained unchanged for 300 million years. It is one of only a few survivors from a group that flourished until about 2 million years ago. Although it is called a crab, the horseshoe is more closely related to spiders than to crustaceans.

recently fossilized shells

Hole bored by predator

Cases for places

IN THE WORLD OF NATURE, being seen or not seen can be the difference between life and death. As creatures move into new environments, or their environment changes, those best suited are naturally selected, and survive. They go through gradual changes, often over millions of years, that permit them to continue to live quite peacefully. Sometimes these are simply changes in habits; but in other cases, creatures evolve the art of camouflage, of being able to blend in with their background, and stay unnoticed by predators, in their chosen habitats. In the shell world, Mother Nature's versatility is displayed in many ways: there are crabs that cover themselves with algae, and molluscs that permanently secure loose objects to their shells. Colour, too, plays an important part in camouflage, and there are many examples of shells that are perfectly designed to blend in with their surroundings. Some molluscs can actually change colour almost instantly, like chameleons. Finally, there are some shells that simply allow themselves to be covered; be it by plant growth, barnacles, or even deposits of lime.

CHAMELEON PRAWN
Cleverly concealed in a sea-lettuce, this prawn changes colour to match the colour of the seaweed on which it is living. At night, however, it always turns a transparent blue colour.

Carrier shell with pebbles

Piece of glass bottle picked up by carrier shell

Coral on which babel's latiaxis lives

Latiaxis encrusted with marine growth

Underside of carrier shell and aperture

Aperture side of coated shell

Cleaned shell

WELCOME ATTACHMENTS
Although barnacles can be a nuisance when stuck to ships, they provide a useful camouflage for the shore crab (above). If the crab keeps still, it looks more like a stone than a living creature.

SHELL COLLECTORS
Carrier shells are so called because some of them can attach a variety of objects to their shells as they grow, ranging from dead shells and coral, to pebbles, and sometimes even bits of garbage left by humans. They live mainly in deep water in most of the world's warm seas.

LIME COATINGS
When alive, most shells are covered with marine encrustations which make them difficult to find underwater. Sometimes, deposits like the limescale found on kitchen utensils can cover a shell entirely. Divers often have trouble locating the latiaxis shells (left). They live on coral, and are often so well disguised that the divers have to feel along the coral surface for the shells with their hands.

Snail in the grass

The colour varieties within land snail shells often seem infinite. The common European banded snail displays enormous variety in its shell colour and pattern, each designed to blend in with its habitat, and protect it from predators.

DECIDUOUS WOODLAND
Brownish-coloured shells without any banding are more likely to go unnoticed by birds and other predators in deciduous woodland areas. The snails often hide among leaf litter on the forest floor.

LONG GRASS
Snails with banded yellow shells usually live on strands of long grass, and manage to look most inconspicuous to predators.

SHORT TURF
From the air, short grass is fairly constant in tone and the yellow, unbanded snail shells that live among the turf are the least noticeable.

BEECH LITTER
In a beech wood, among the leaf litter, heavily-banded shells often occur. The banding density varies according to the type of litter the snails live in.

Settlers on the sands

Unlike a rocky coastline or coral reef (pp. 46-53), a sandy shore seems to offer little shelter for shelled creatures. However, in order to avoid being exposed, many of the animals found on sandy shores are burrowers, sometimes spending their entire lives buried deep below the surface. When a sandy beach is exposed at low tide it seems a lifeless, apparently barren environment, but close inspection will reveal a variety of holes, mounds and tracks - all evidence of animals that have dug down to where moisture is retained until the next tide. Sometimes hundreds of shells may be living in an area of sand no larger than this page.

Necklace shells

Saint James' scallop

FLAT-SIDE-UP
Scallops are sought-after food (see p. 35), and the scallop shell is the symbol of Saint James, the fisherman. The two valves of Saint James's scallop are very different in shape: the bottom valve, commonly put to use as an ashtray, is convex (domed), while the top valve is flattened. The scallops lie with their bottom valve buried in the sand.

NECKLACE SHELLS
Necklace shells are so called because they lay their eggs in coiled, strap-like bands. These gastropod molluscs are common predators that plough through the sand in search of food. They drill circular holes in bivalve shells to eat the animals inside.

SANDY EXPANSES
The long stretches of sandy beach that occur on many coasts are formed by waves, tides, and currents. Sea cliffs are eroded by waves and weather, and the rock, mixed with shells, is broken into tiny particles. This mixture eventually ends up as sand; on-shore as a beach, and off-shore as a sand-bar or bank.

SUNDIAL SHELLS
These gastropods, also known as "architecture shells", have elegant spiral shells and are found on tropical sandy shores. Some sundial shells measure just a few millimetres in diameter and live in very deep water.

Tropical sundials

MARGIN SHELLS
These colourful shells can be found on the sandy shores of many warm countries. Empty specimens found washed up on the beach do not usually have the naturally polished look of living shells.

West African margin shells

SPOTTED DIGGERS
These colourful acteon shells burrow into the sand using their flattened, spade-like heads. Acteon shells can be found in many of the world's seas; these two are of a type only recently discovered in the Persian Gulf.

Eloise's acteon

BUBBLES AND CANOES
Bubble and canoe shells are closely related molluscs that occur in a variety of marine environments. They "toboggan" along the surface of fine mud in search of small molluscs that they eat by crushing them with their powerful gizzards (stomachs). The animals are often many times larger than their fragile, inflated shells.

Bubble shell

Canoe bubble shell

BURROWING BIVALVES
The majority of shells found on sandy shores are bivalves. The Mediterranean scraper solecurtus and the Indo-Pacific sunset siliqua are typical of bivalve shells that use their muscles to pull themselves deep into the sand when the tide goes out.

Sunset siliqua

Scraper solecurtus

Razor shell

Junonia volute

KEEPING A TOE-HOLD
The oddly-shaped Pelican's foot shell lives on muddy gravel below the low-tide mark. Its shelly "toes" seem to serve as an anchorage in this soft base. These common shells were widely collected in the 19th century for use in "shell art".

Pelican's foot shell

BORING SHELL
This Marlinspike shell is the largest of a group of shells called "augers" - named after a tool used for boring into the ground. These long and slender shells are found mainly on tropical beaches and are perfectly adapted for digging in the sand.

Marlinspike auger

TUSK-LIKE TUBES
These "shells" resemble those of tusk shells (p. 18) but are in fact tubes of sand sculpted by certain marine worms. The grains of sand are bound together by mucus secreted by the worm, and the tubes lie buried in the sand, with only the worm's tentacled head appearing above the surface.

Worm tube made from sand

INDIAN SCREW SHELL
The multi-whorled turritella, or screw shell, burrows into muddy gravel by moving jerkily from side to side, using its shell as a digging tool.

THE JUNONIA
This volute shell (see p. 13) lives in sand off the southeast United States. A large and colourful shell, it is highly prized by shell collectors.

SPINDLE SHELL
The high-spired spindle shell is another sand-burrowing predatory mollusc. These shells occur in most of the world's warmer seas, some tropical types reaching lengths of over 20 cm (8 in).

The Marlinspike Auger can grow 15-20 cm (6-8 in) long

Indian turritella

East African spindle shell

A SHARP MOVER
Shaped like old-style "cut-throat" razors, and often nearly as sharp, these bivalve molluscs can burrow deep into the sand very rapidly, using their wedge-shaped foot to pull the shell downwards. The two razor shell valves are joined by a strong ligament, and the valves of dead animals can often be found still attached to each other.

Exhalant siphon

Inhalant siphon

Hairs on antennae interlock to form breathing tube

LIFE DOWN UNDER
The burrowing molluscs breathe and feed through long extensions called "siphons". Each lives at its own depth, some near the surface, others deep down, and their siphons may be extremely long. The overall length of some bivalve molluscs can be 4-5 times that of their shells. Some crustaceans also live below the sand; the masked crab digs down with its legs so that only the tips of its long antennae protrude above the surface during the day. It only appears to forage for food at night.

Male masked crab

Masked crab

Razor shell

Tusk shell

Tellin

Sand gaper

Muscular foot for burrowing

COVERING CLAWS
The Calappa crab is one of many crabs that have claws specially adapted to cover themselves with sand, rather than burrowing deep into it.

Calappa crab

Female masked crab

Pelican's foot shell

Foliate tellin

Continued on next page

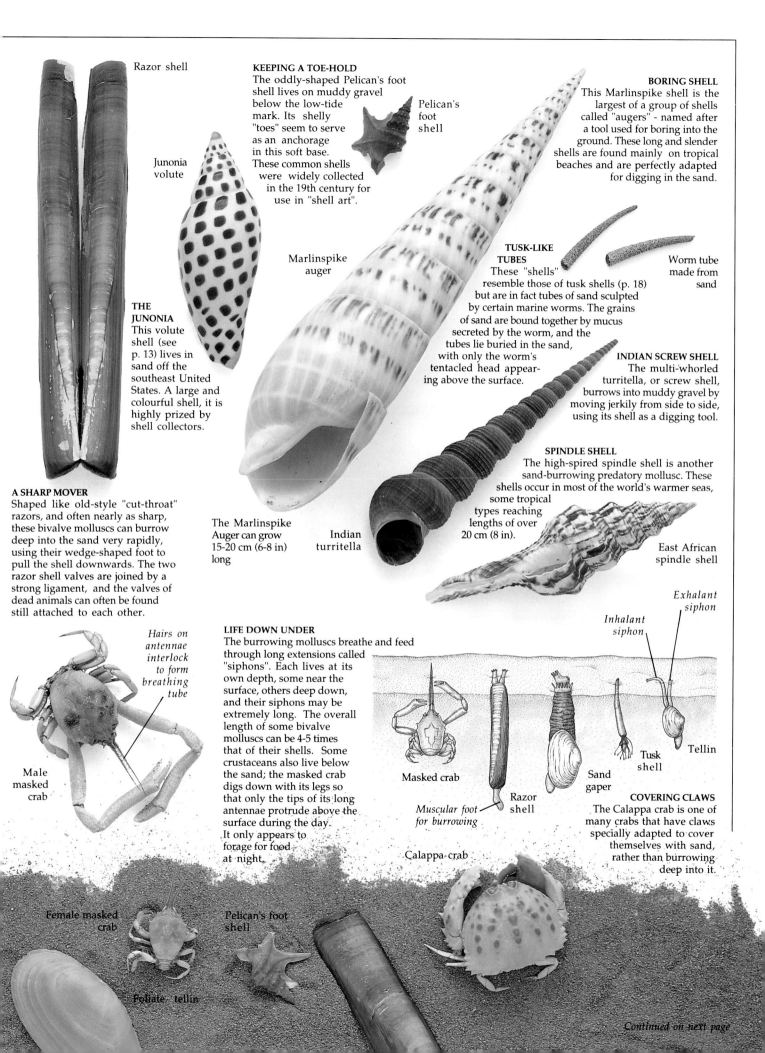

PREYING MANTIS

The large mantis shrimp is unlikely to be found on the beach, as it usually lives below tidal levels. Its thin, light shell allows it to move quickly along the seabed in pursuit of prey, which it crushes with its front legs. In parts of the Mediterranean, this shrimp is fished commercially for food.

Spiny crushers

Mantis shrimp

SINGLE-CELLED SHELLS

Looking at sand through a microscope reveals the shells of many types of marine creatures. Among the most common are the strangely shaped, single-celled creatures known as Foraminifera, which live at all depths of the oceans. Some areas of the sea floor are made up of millions upon millions of these tiny shells.

Stichostega

Helixostega

Entomostega

MINIATURE MOLLUSCS

Mollusc shells come in all shapes and sizes. Sometimes sand is made up almost entirely of small shells and shell fragments. Perfectly formed miniatures of the snail shells shown on the previous page can be found among the sand on many beaches.

SMALL-FRY

Prawns and shrimps occur in many types of marine environment, often in great numbers. When disturbed they are able to shoot backwards with a swift movement of their tailfan. Shrimps use their legs and long feelers to bury themselves in the sand, with just the shorter pair of antennae poking out to detect nearby prey.

Antennae

Walking legs

Shrimp

Prawn

Dark blotches to discourage predators attacking from behind

Tail fan

Paddle-like appendages for swimming

THE STORY OF SAND

There are many different types of sand, but all of them are by-products of weathering and erosion by the waves. Rock particles, broken shells, and fish skeletons, glass and pieces of coral, all are deposited on to beaches, and continually worn down to tiny grains by wave movement.

GIANT SANDMAN

The sand that makes up deserts on dry land is often formed through the wind erosion of rocks. Some desert sand, however, was formed by water erosion and deposited by the oceans many millions of years ago. The Sphinx and the great pyramids of Egypt are all built from sandstone, which contains the fossilized shells of billions of minute marine creatures known as "nummulites".

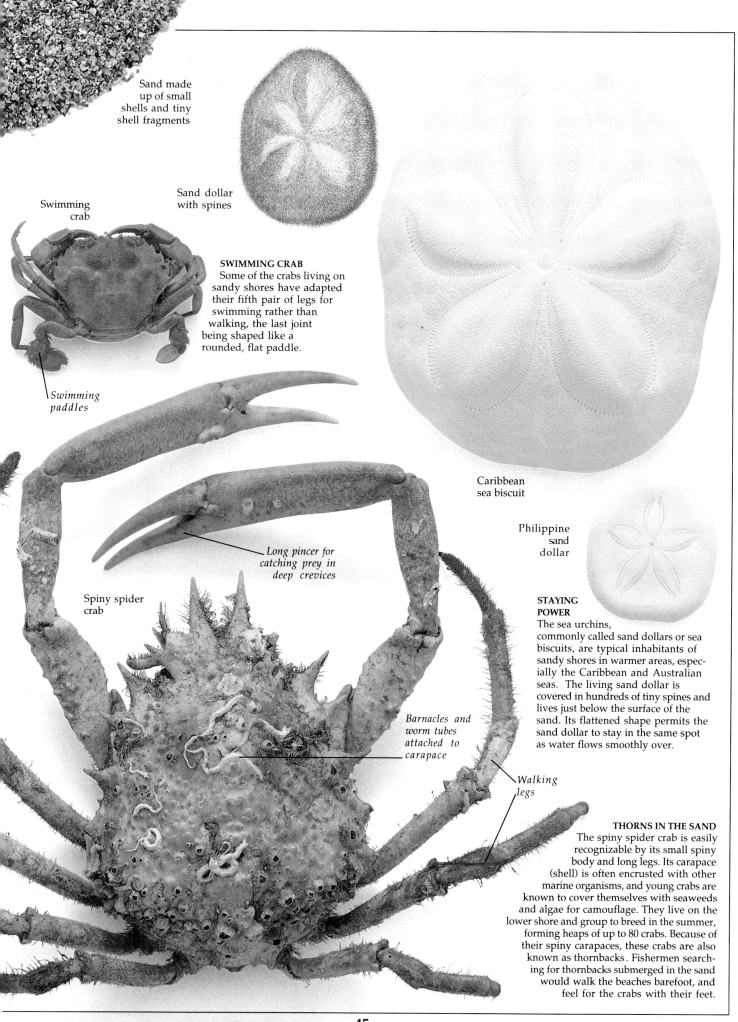

Sand made up of small shells and tiny shell fragments

Sand dollar with spines

Swimming crab

SWIMMING CRAB
Some of the crabs living on sandy shores have adapted their fifth pair of legs for swimming rather than walking, the last joint being shaped like a rounded, flat paddle.

Swimming paddles

Caribbean sea biscuit

Philippine sand dollar

Long pincer for catching prey in deep crevices

Spiny spider crab

Barnacles and worm tubes attached to carapace

STAYING POWER
The sea urchins, commonly called sand dollars or sea biscuits, are typical inhabitants of sandy shores in warmer areas, especially the Caribbean and Australian seas. The living sand dollar is covered in hundreds of tiny spines and lives just below the surface of the sand. Its flattened shape permits the sand dollar to stay in the same spot as water flows smoothly over.

Walking legs

THORNS IN THE SAND
The spiny spider crab is easily recognizable by its small spiny body and long legs. Its carapace (shell) is often encrusted with other marine organisms, and young crabs are known to cover themselves with seaweeds and algae for camouflage. They live on the lower shore and group to breed in the summer, forming heaps of up to 80 crabs. Because of their spiny carapaces, these crabs are also known as thornbacks. Fishermen searching for thornbacks submerged in the sand would walk the beaches barefoot, and feel for the crabs with their feet.

Life on the rocks

ROCKY SHORES provide a diverse and complex environment for many types of marine creatures. The types of rock from which a beach is made, its position in relation to the sea, and the range of tide levels all play a part in determining the variety of creatures that live there. The tide may expose the rocky shore for several hours each day, and some creatures have built up a tolerance to living without water for extended periods. Those that have not managed to reach deeper waters or find tidal pools when the water recedes, will dry out and die from exposure to the air and sun. These are not the only elements to which a rocky shore may be exposed; the pounding of powerful waves erodes the rocks themselves. Many animals living on the rocks have evolved very strong shells that can withstand the force of the waves, and many have developed ways of anchoring themselves firmly to the surface of the rocks, so they are not washed away. The rocky seabed plays host to an even wider range of creatures, many of which spend much of their lives hidden in holes or even underneath rocks.

ROCK POOL INHABITANTS
Life can be hard in the shallow water pools left by receding tides. Many creatures that prefer less light and warmth are left stranded and must try their best to find shelter.

BOUVIER'S CRAB
Like many small crabs, this one lives between or under rocks, and only emerges to scavenge for food at night.

Bearded ark shell

BEARDED ARK SHELL
So called because of the tiny hairs that cover its shell, this is a bivalve that lives in rock crevices, attaching itself by means of a broad byssus (see left). The shell of this creature is often distorted as it grows to fit snugly into its rocky niche.

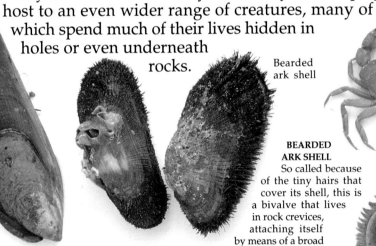

New Zealand mussel

Mussel with byssal threads

Common blue mussels

Tail fan

MUSSELS WITH ANCHORS
Mussels are common inhabitants of many rocky shores, often living in massive clusters high on the shore. Mussels anchor themselves to rocks and other surfaces by means of byssal threads: strong, thin filaments planted by the mussel's foot.

THE JEWEL IN THE SHELL
This rough star-shell lives on the rocky shores of the Mediterranean, but is found below tide level. The shell is often heavily encrusted with marine growths. The bright-red operculum is sometimes used to make jewellery.

Operculum

WINKLES ON THE WEEDS
The tiny periwinkles are among the most common inhabitants of rocky shores. They tend to live high up on the shore, clinging to rocks and clumps of seaweed.

Rough
periwinkles

Antenna

Claw

*Common
shore crab*

COMMON CRAB
The shore crab is one of the most common European crabs, and can be found lurking under rocks and seaweed.

ELUSIVE LOBSTER
The common lobster is highly prized for food, and is a favourite catch for divers. Lobsters can be difficult to find as they blend in with their surroundings, and often hide away in crevices during the day, with only their claws and antennae showing.

Walking legs

STONY-SHELLED CRAB
The Mediterranean stone crab is so called because of its heavy-looking, irregular shell.

Continued from previous page

Holes for
expulsion of
water and
waste

COLOURFUL EAR SHELLS
Abalones, or ormers, like this Californian
green abalone, are also known as ear
shells because of their shape. The
row of holes in the shell allows
water and waste to be passed
out. Beautifully iridescent
within, these shells are used
to make jewellery, and the
animals inside are often
eaten (see p. 34).

Lamellose
ormer

BARNACLE ROCK SHELL
This odd-looking shell
found off the coasts of Peru
and Chile is related to the
murex shells (p. 12), but sits on
rocks, much like a limpet (see below).

Chiton shells
(see p. 18)

LONG-LASTING LIMPETS
Limpets are renowned for
holding on tightly to
rocks, so as not
to be knocked off
by strong waves.
They have had a
magnetic mine
that clings to
ships' hulls
named after
them. Limpet
shells are usually
either very eroded
or covered with algae
and other forms of
marine life.

Barnacles
and algae on
limpet shell

Safian
limpet
shell

KILLER SNAILS
Most rocky shores play host
to snails that feed on
bivalves such as mus-
sels and oysters. Some
"drill" into the shells
of their prey, while
others, like the Pana-
manian thorn latirus,
have developed a special
tooth that helps to break
open the shells.

Thorn
latirus

Tooth

Sting
winkle

European
china
limpet

Rock-boring shells

Some shelled creatures have overcome the problem of being washed away by strong waves by sticking to rocks permanently, or even boring into them. These animals feed by extending tubes or fans out from their shells to catch prey, or by opening their valves and allowing the current to bring their microscopic food source to them. The creatures that hide away in holes in the rocks are not only safe from being washed away, but are also protected from most of their enemies.

BURROWING SEA URCHINS
Certain types of sea urchin use their spines to dig out holes in sand, mud, or rocks. This protects them from the force of waves or currents. They hold on to the rock with their rows of suckered tube feet.

Limestone   *Shell*

READY-MADE HOMES
Retzius shells settle in holes that already exist in rocks, but the animal enlarges its home as it grows. Eventually, it becomes firmly wedged in, making it impossible for the shell to be dislodged by the waves.

Calcareous tube

GIVE-AWAY TUBE
Some of the creatures that live inside rocks are only visible because of a shelly tube, which they extend from their hidden niche.

Top valve of shell

STUCK LIKE GLUE
The jewel-box shell is a bivalve that does not live inside the rock, but cements its lower valve to the surface, in the same way as some types of oyster.

DIGGING DOWN DEEP
The piddock shell can be found buried in a variety of hard substances, which it bores into mechanically with its two valves. Some types of piddock can live up to 1 m (3 ft) below the surface.

Piddock shell removed from rock

Piddock hole in rock

Date mussel removed from rock

Piddock shell and siphon

Shell embedded in rock

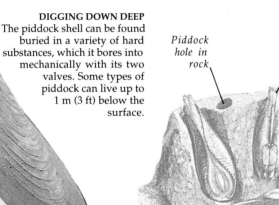

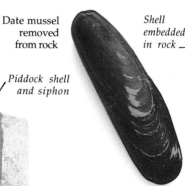

ROCK EROSION
Unlike the piddock, date mussels do not bore holes mechanically. Instead they secrete a special chemical that softens the rock, so that it can be easily scraped away and flushed out by using water currents from the mussel's siphons. Date mussels are edible.

SHELLS UPON SHELLS
Shells that spend their lives stuck to one spot frequently provide suitable homes for other shells. White shelly tubes belonging to a certain type of marine worm are often seen on rocks and other shells.

Worm tubes on thorny oyster

BLISTERING BARNACLES
Barnacles are often found in massive colonies clinging to a rocky shoreline. They also attach themselves to the undersides of boats, and have to be scraped off so they don't slow the boat down.

Cluster of barnacles

WHERE'S THE WORM?
Although commonly called worm shells, these irregularly shaped tubes belong to gastropod molluscs, which spend their lives cemented to hard surfaces.

Worm shells on rock

Worm tubes on Mediterranean blue mussel shell

Residents of the reefs

CORAL REEFS ARE COMPLEX NETWORKS of millions of living marine organisms, supporting more life than any other type of marine environment. They are like underwater gardens, incorporating a wide variety of different colours and textures, and very much dependent on sunlight and warmth for survival. Most coral occurs in warm regions of the world, many large coral outcrops being found in the Caribbean, off West Africa and throughout the Indo-Pacific. Some outcrops are huge, the most famous being Australia's Great Barrier Reef, which stretches for over 2,000 km (1,250 miles). Among the multitude of animals inhabiting the reefs are many shelled creatures, although they may be difficult to spot, hiding away under or between the corals during the day. Not until the relative safety of darkness do they emerge in search of food. The shallow-water corals and the life they support is extremely vulnerable, and although many coral reefs were established long before humans existed on earth, they are now being threatened by human predation and pollution.

LEGENDS OF THE REEFS
Mermaids and sea-nymphs are legendary creatures thought by ancient sailors to inhabit the seas around coral reefs. They are often depicted as using the spiny shell of a murex to comb their long tresses.

Violet coral shell

VIOLET CORAL SHELL
This little shell is a typical inhabitant of tropical reefs, usually living in crevices or hollows of live coral heads. Females of this species are often larger than males.

Princely cone

Marble cone

CONES AND MITRES
Some of the largest and most decorative mollusc shells of the coral reefs are the cone and mitre shells. Although they belong to different families, both types of shells are known for their bright colours and patterns. Cone shells are also renowned for their ability to shoot a paralyzing dart into their prey. This phenomenon is known to have been lethal.

Fluted growth-layers

FLUTED FILTER FEEDER
A smaller relative of the giant clam (p. 17) which grows to over 1.5 m (5 ft) in length, this pretty clam shell can be found on shallow reefs throughout most of the Indo-Pacific area. It is a filter feeder, lying with its valves apart and sifting out the micro-organisms from the water.

Papal mitre

COLOURFUL COWRIES
Among the prettiest and most diverse creatures to be found on the reefs are the popular cowrie shells. The smaller types are often found living on the underside of coral slabs.

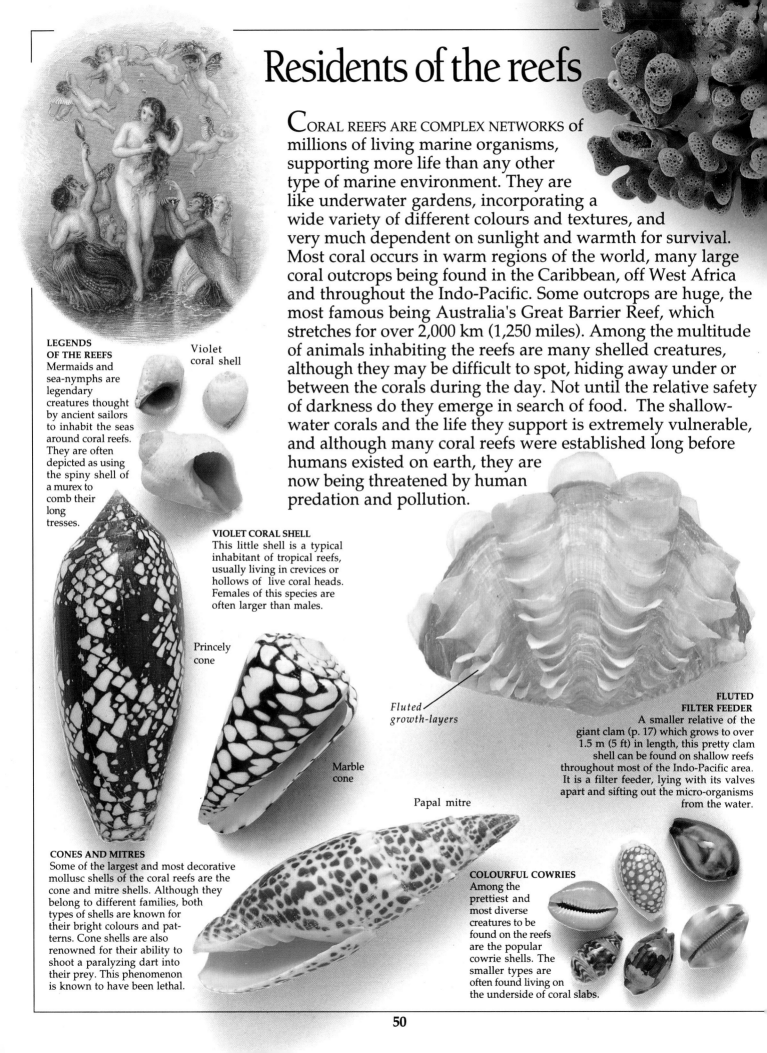

Blue coral

Oldest whorls of shell

Brachiopod

Scorpion murex

Jewel-box shells

SECURE SUPPORT
Cemented firmly in place, jewel-box shells and a brachiopod form a micro-community on this piece of Atlantic coral.

Zambo's murex

BURROWING CORAL SHELLS
One of the most unusual shells inhabiting the reef is the burrowing coral shell, which spends its life deeply embedded in brain coral. As the mollusc grows, it slowly builds a long, irregular tube and fills the oldest whorls with shelly matter.

Map cowrie

Mole cowrie

ADAPTING TO LIFE ON THE REEF
Many of the murex shells that live around the reefs are shaped as if to mimic the coral itself. The living shells are often heavily encrusted with marine growth, which provides excellent camouflage. The scorpio conch also has distinctive "spines", which permit it to crawl on the sand around the reef without being swept away by strong underwater currents.

Scorpio conch

COLLECTORS' PIECES
The obvious beauty and relative ease with which most cowries can be found on a shallow-water reef make them targets for shell collectors. Unfortunately, indiscriminate collecting on the more accessible reefs in the Pacific has threatened many once-thriving populations. The demand for these shells has encouraged collecting as a full-time occupation in some areas of the tropics.

Eyed cowrie

Turtle cowrie

COLOURLESS CORAL CORPSE
The "coral" that many people recognize is usually just a bleached, white skeleton of what was once a massive community of tiny, brightly-coloured creatures known as polyps. Coral comes in all shapes and sizes, and shells can often be found hidden underneath or embedded within the fragile structure of both living and dead coral. Although all corals are decorative, it is usually the deep-water forms that are fished for use in jewellery.

51

Continued on next page

BORN OF THE OCEAN
Rising out of the sea, Erskine Island off Queensland, Australia, is made from dead coral and surrounded by living coral. Thousands of tiny coral islands like this one can be found on Australia's Great Barrier Reef.

Colour range in tests of tropical sea urchins

TROPICAL TURTLES
Marine turtles can sometimes be seen in the warm waters surrounding tropical coral reefs. The hawksbill turtle (p. 31) is a typical coral-reef dweller. Because of the abundance of marine life, shallow-water reefs are ideal feeding grounds for many types of creature. Some marine turtles have developed incredible migratory habits, for example travelling hundreds of miles from their feeding grounds to nest on the beaches where they were born. The green turtle (below) travels to its nesting ground every two or three years .

Green turtle

SPINY REEF DWELLERS
Common inhabitants of most coral reefs are the sea urchins (p. 20), their spine-covered tests usually found in reef hollows. The sea urchins are mainly herbivorous, feeding on tiny algae that they scrape off rock and dead coral.

CARNIVOROUS PLANT?
These strange-looking specimens may look like plants but are in fact polyps, like corals. This straw tubularia is a carnivorous polyp with long stems encased in yellowish tubes. These creatures attach themselves readily to shells and stones.

Smooth laminae do not overlap

Colour of shell can be green, brown, or black

Skeleton of
brain coral

BRAIN OR MUSHROOM?
Two of the most common types of coral found in tropical
areas are brain corals and mushroom corals. From the
pictures, it is not difficult to see why they got their
names! Brain corals, made by a colony containing millions
of minute coral polyps, grow into a heap with patterning
like the folds found on brains. The smaller mushroom
corals are disc-like, look almost edible, and, because they
are not attached to a hard base, can move short distances.

Skeleton of
mushroom
coral

Living brain
coral in front
of sea fan

Crustaceans and corals

The crustaceans have successfully made homes for
themselves in coral reefs, as they have in all marine
environments. Crabs, lobsters, and shrimps can be
found there in great variety. Some,
such as the coral-gall crab (below),
actually live inside the coral; others
display bright colours or unusual
shapes that help them to blend in
with the coral garden.

CORAL-DWELLING CRAB
The coral-gall crab settles on coral
when very young and becomes en-
veloped as the coral grows.

A LIVING PEARL
With its knobbly shell, the
tropical spotted rock crab, or
pearl crab (below), is easily
recognizable.

Galls on the living coral

**NOW YOU
SEE IT...**
The ghost crab is so called because it is the same colour as the
sandy tropical beaches where it
lives, and seems to appear and
disappear at random.

Deep-sea dwellers

A SURPRISING AMOUNT OF THE EARTH'S SURFACE - about 70 per cent - is under water, covered by the oceans. The sea plunges to great depths off the world's land-masses - in some areas to over 11,000 metres (33,500 ft). With this huge amount of water, it is little wonder that the ocean depths are among the least-known, most mysterious areas of our planet. By contrast with the seabed near the coast, which is covered with rocks and jungles of seaweed, the floor of the deep sea is barren; covered with a type of soft grey ooze. Deep-sea explorers and fishermen are constantly dredging up previously unknown types of sea-creature. The deep-sea-dwelling shelled creatures mainly belong to the groups that we know from coastal, more shallow waters; the molluscs, crustaceans, and echinoderms. Almost everything that dies in the oceans eventually drifts down to the seabed to form matter known as detritus, and most deep-sea creatures feed by extracting nutrients from this.

LIGHT OF THE DEPTHS
Many deep-sea creatures have evolved methods that make them glow. This light, known as bioluminescence, is seen above in tiny crustaceans, called ostracods.

Victor Dan's delphinula (Philippines)

Hirase's slit shell (Japan)

Sunburst star turban (New Zealand)

Yoka star turban (Japan)

Margarite shell (Taiwan)

Deep-sea gastropods

Shells found in deep water, where there is no light, tend to be less colourful than those, for instance, from coral reefs. However, there is no shortage of beauty or variety among deep-sea gastropods. Most of the examples above were once thought to be extremely rare, but as fishing techniques improve, more and more specimens are being found. The delphinula shell (top left) was discovered only recently in the Philippines.

UNDERWATER LAMPS
The transparent, glassy lamp-shells (right) are typical of many deep-sea dwellers, because they are not brightly coloured. Some 300 different types of lampshell exist, and many of them live in deep water They attach them-selves to solid bases by using a muscular stalk.

Mediterranean lampshells

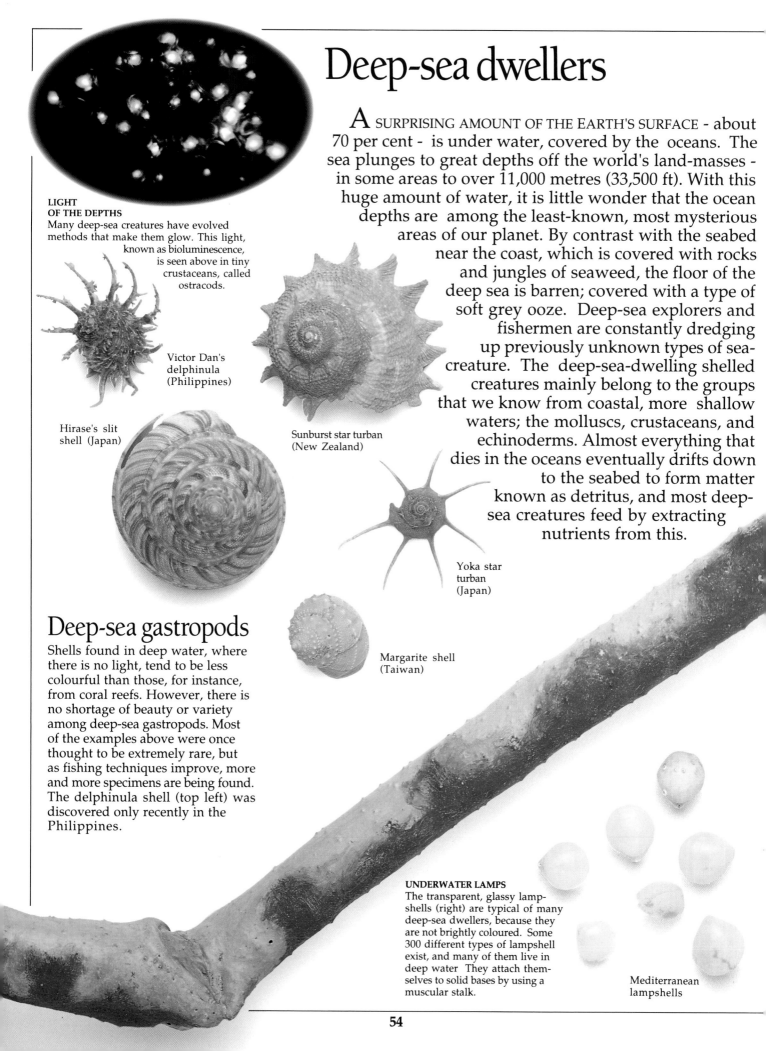

Deep-sea crustacea

Crustaceans are among the most abundant of creatures to be found in deep water. They range from tiny ostracods (left-hand page) to massive crabs, like the Japanese spider crab (leg shown below), and blind deep-sea lobsters whose fossils were known long before living examples were found. Some of the larger crustaceans are fished by laying traps, but most of them live a tranquil life in the darkness of the seabed, out of human reach.

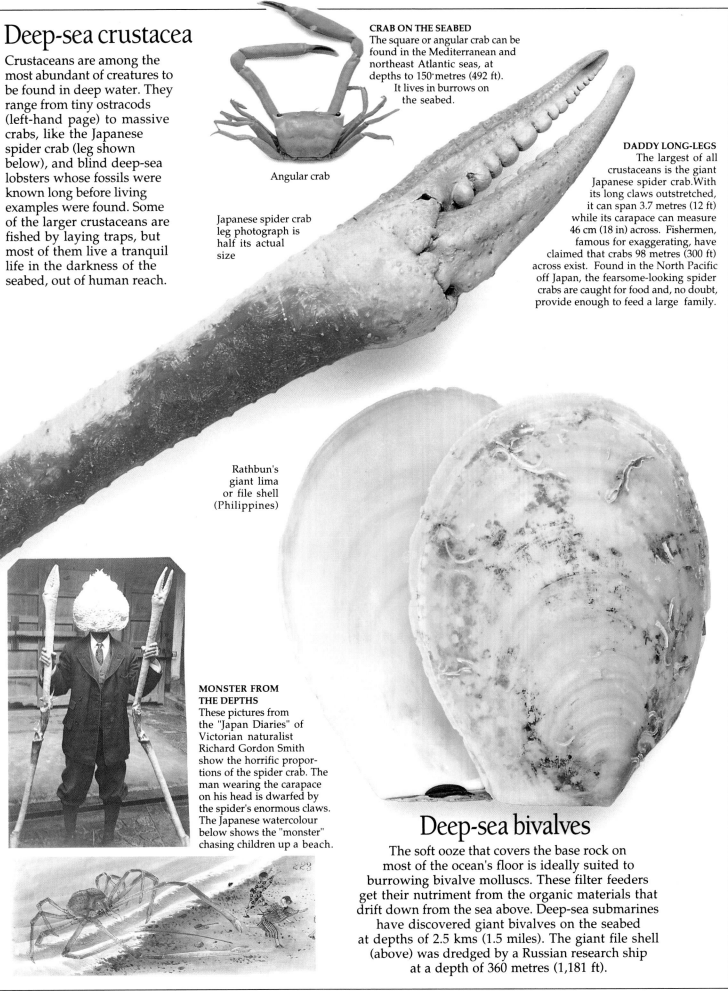

CRAB ON THE SEABED
The square or angular crab can be found in the Mediterranean and northeast Atlantic seas, at depths to 150 metres (492 ft). It lives in burrows on the seabed.

Angular crab

Japanese spider crab leg photograph is half its actual size

DADDY LONG-LEGS
The largest of all crustaceans is the giant Japanese spider crab.With its long claws outstretched, it can span 3.7 metres (12 ft) while its carapace can measure 46 cm (18 in) across. Fishermen, famous for exaggerating, have claimed that crabs 98 metres (300 ft) across exist. Found in the North Pacific off Japan, the fearsome-looking spider crabs are caught for food and, no doubt, provide enough to feed a large family.

Rathbun's giant lima or file shell (Philippines)

MONSTER FROM THE DEPTHS
These pictures from the "Japan Diaries" of Victorian naturalist Richard Gordon Smith show the horrific proportions of the spider crab. The man wearing the carapace on his head is dwarfed by the spider's enormous claws. The Japanese watercolour below shows the "monster" chasing children up a beach.

Deep-sea bivalves

The soft ooze that covers the base rock on most of the ocean's floor is ideally suited to burrowing bivalve molluscs. These filter feeders get their nutriment from the organic materials that drift down from the sea above. Deep-sea submarines have discovered giant bivalves on the seabed at depths of 2.5 kms (1.5 miles). The giant file shell (above) was dredged by a Russian research ship at a depth of 360 metres (1,181 ft).

Freshwater finds

THE VARIETY OF LIFE in freshwater habitats, such as rivers and estuaries, is not as great as in the world's seas. All freshwater creatures began life in the sea, and developed from marine creatures millions of years ago. Many belong to the same families that live today in marine environments. The freshwater crustaceans, molluscs, and turtles all have bodies which successfully adapted to freshwater life. Their habits have adapted, too, in order to go upstream from the seas and maintain their ground against the constant flow of water and strong currents. Many freshwater creatures lay eggs that can be secured to plants, or give birth to live young - the free-swimming larvae common to many sea creatures would have no chance of survival, and would be washed away downstream towards the sea.

Chinese mitten crab

A CRAB WITH MITTENS
Some types of crab live both in pure freshwater and in low salt-water environments like estuaries and mangrove swamps. The Chinese mitten crab, or woolly-handed crab, above, lives in estuaries of the Orient. With its characteristic furry cuff, it is is easy to see how it got its name!

FRESHWATER LOBSTER
Crayfish live in freshwater habitats in many parts of the world - in Australia, they can be found in dams and are known as "yabbies". Sometimes fished for food, these crustaceans tend to live under stones or in shallow burrows. Most crayfish will lie low until a small fish or some other tempting morsel passes by, and then will snap it up in their powerful claws. Not all crayfish are active the whole year round - some dig deep burrows in which they remain all winter; others swim out to deeper waters and lie on the bottom.

Madagascan crayfish

Murray river crayfish

Underside of a crayfish

English crayfish

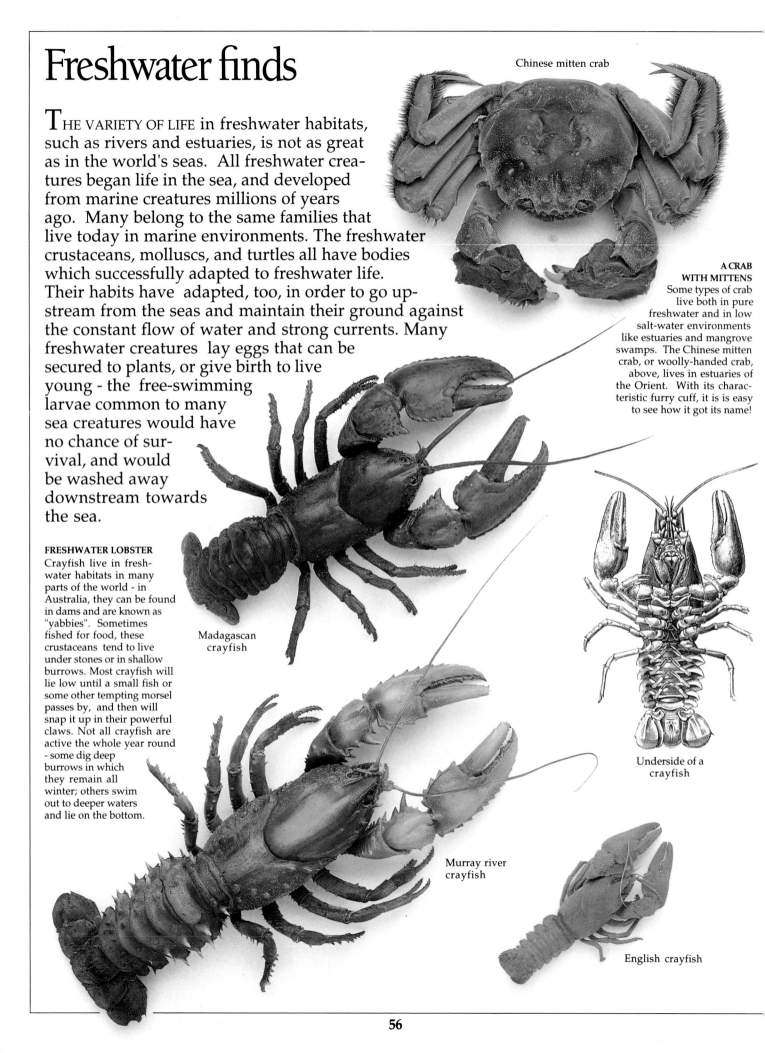

A REAL SOFTIE
While most members of the tortoise family have hardened carapaces, the spiny soft-shelled river turtle from North America has a rounded, flexible carapace with no bony plates at all. Unlike other members of its family, the softshell is able to move fast both in water and on land.

TURTLE OR TERRAPIN?
The only real difference between a turtle and a terrapin is its habitat. The European pond turtle is one of over 80 species of mainly freshwater turtles living today. A carnivorous turtle, it hunts both in the water and on land, feeding on small fish, worms, molluscs, and frogs.

European pond turtle

SNAPPING, NOT NAPPING
The alligator snapping turtle is one of the most bizarre-looking of all the turtles. It catches prey by lying totally still on the riverbed, huge mouth agape. Within its mouth is a fleshy, pink appendage that looks like a wriggling worm. Any unsuspecting fish that takes this "bait" finds instant death between the turtle's powerful, snapping jaws. The alligator snapping turtles inhabit deep rivers and lakes of central North America, where they are often caught for food (see right).

Alligator snapping turtle farm

South American ramshorn snails

Giant Amazonian river snail

Giant Venezuelan river snail

African freshwater "oyster"

FRESHWATER MOLLUSCS
Molluscs living in freshwater environments tend to have lighter, thinner shells than marine ones and are less colourful, enabling them to blend in well with their surroundings. Freshwater gastropods come in all shapes and sizes, the largest ones being the river snails of Amazonia and some areas of Africa (see above). Gastropods and bivalves are the only types of mollusc that live in freshwater.

Inland inhabitants

ALTHOUGH MOST KINDS OF SHELLED CREATURE have their homes in the world's oceans, there are some that, over millions of years, have emerged slowly from the sea and evolved to cope with living on land. Among the most successful of these creatures are the molluscs, including many thousands of different types of land snail that live in environments as diverse as deserts and tropical rainforests. Some live high up in branches of the forest canopy, while others can be found living several feet underground. A few crustaceans and some reptiles also have adapted successfully to the land, although the slow-moving tortoises are the only reptiles that have needed to keep a protective outer shell.

Coconut husk broken by robber crab

Powerful claws

Strengthened carapace

CRABS IN THE TREES
The robber or "coconut" crab can be found on some Pacific islands. A tree-climbing giant, it can grow up to 45 cm (18 in) long and climbs trees in search of coconuts, which it cracks open with its powerful claws. As a young adult, the crab carries a mollusc shell, like a hermit crab, and when it has outgrown this, it carries half a coconut! Eventually, it relies on its claws and hardened exoskeleton for protection. On some islands, the crab is hunted for food. When caught, however, the robber crab must be held carefully to avoid serious injury, as the Cook Islander is demonstrating (left).

Common
woodlouse

ARMOURED LOUSE
Of all the crustacea, the most
completetly adapted to
terrestrial life are the
woodlice. They can be found in
every garden, under stones or
flower-pots. Woodlice
congregate in damp or humid
spots, feeding on decaying
vegetable matter and, of
course, rotting wood.

*Starry pattern
on carapace
laminae*

STARRY SHELL
Unlike their relatives the
turtles and terrapins, most
tortoises live on land. Like
these aquatic cousins, tortoises
carry a shell or carapace on top of
their bodies. Made from bony plates
known as laminae, a tortoise's shell
often displays quite beautiful
patterns. This starred tortoise ,
from India and Sri Lanka, is so
called because of the striking
geometric patterns on its carapace, very much like little
black and yellow stars.

Tree bark

*Sharply pointed
feet help robber
crab to climb*

A Japanese
tortoise
charmer -
safer than
snakes!

A snail emerges

Not famed for their mobility or speed,
land snails are in fact quite versatile
when they need to be. These
photographs illustrate how a snail
uses its strong muscles to right its shell.

A sudden jerk
of the mollusc
corrects the shell's
position

Removed from its
resting place, the
mollusc hides
within its shell to
protect its soft body

The snail's foot
begins to emerge
tentatively, taking
in its new
surroundings

As the foot emerges,
the changing
distribution of weight
rocks the shell over

The entire foot of the
snail is now out and
the head is directed
under the shell

Its foot fully
extended, the
snail steams off
at full speed

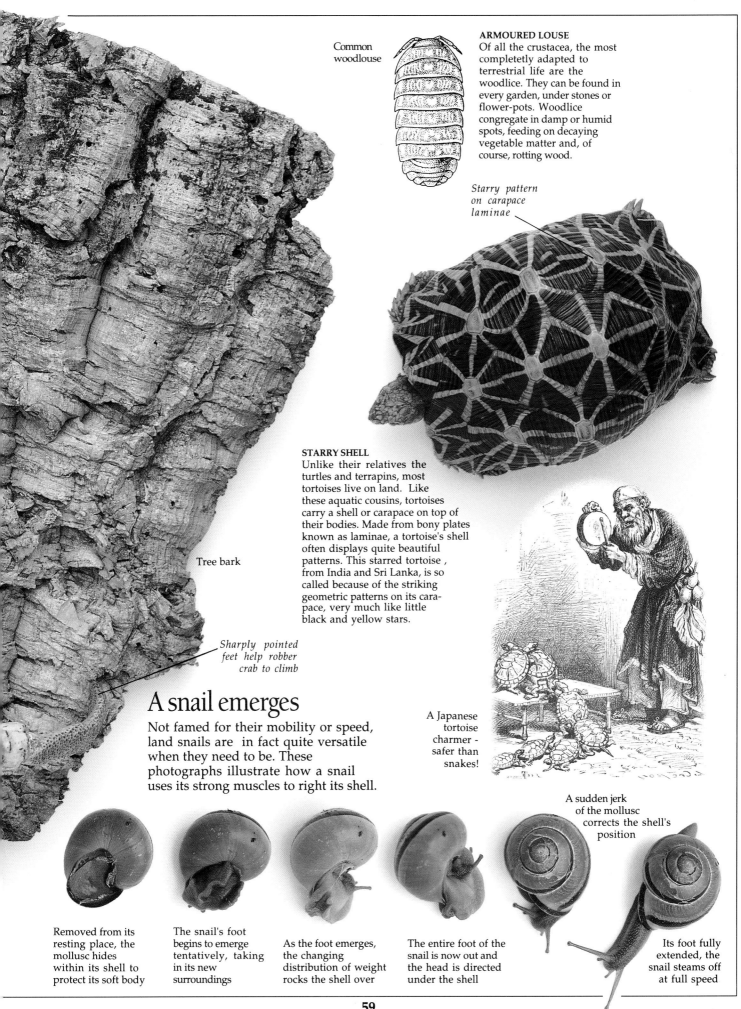

Shells in strange places

IN THE CONSTANT STRUGGLE FOR SURVIVAL, plants and animals have evolved to occupy a great variety of land, freshwater, and marine environments. In the world of shelled creatures, there are many examples of peculiar habitats that are occupied only by one type of shelled animal, and many have learned that the best way to survive is not to be too fussy - barnacles and some types of worm are among the creatures that are concerned only with having a solid base on which to live. Some have developed close associations with other creatures and exist parasitically, while others will cling to almost any secure surface they can find.

Brachiopod or lampshell

LINGERING LAMPSHELL
Brachiopods, or lampshells, attach themselves to solid substrates by means of a flexible stalk, and can sometimes be found living on mollusc shells, as here.

COCKLE COLONY
Covering this empty cockle shell are hundreds of white shelly tubes made by a type of marine worm. These worms attach themselves to almost any solid surface available, and often live in large colonies. They extend their tentacles from the end of the tubes to catch particles of food that float past.

Calcareous worm tubes

Barnacles

Worm tube on a topshell

Mollusc

Mollusc shell

IN A SPIN
As if wanting to mimic its shelled partner, this worm tube has slowly followed the spiral coiling of the mollusc on which it sits.

MIXED MOLLUSCS
This bivalve mollusc, a thorny oyster, has two very different types of marine animal attached to its shell. Although the white shelly tubes are all worm-shaped, the largest one actually belongs to a gastropod mollusc.

Worm tubes

SITTING ON THE POT
Submerged underwater for about 2,000 years, this Roman two-handled jar (right) has probably played host to thousands of different marine creatures. There are three distinct types visible here: barnacles, worm tubes, and molluscs.

Goose barnacles

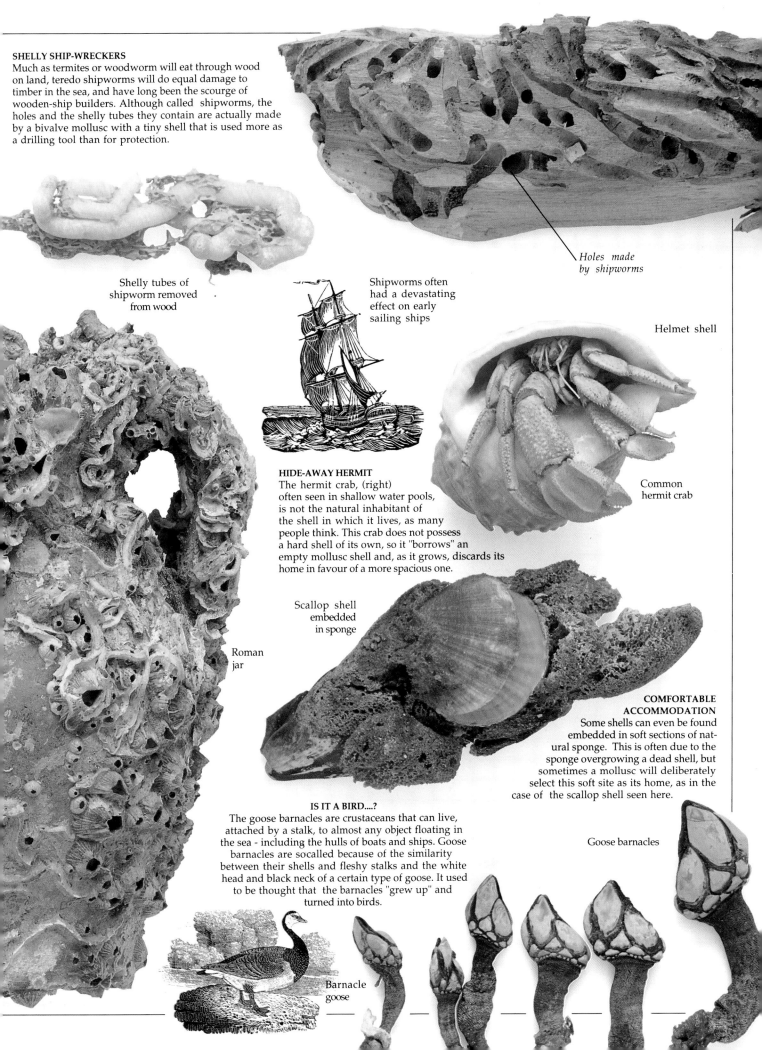

SHELLY SHIP-WRECKERS
Much as termites or woodworm will eat through wood on land, teredo shipworms will do equal damage to timber in the sea, and have long been the scourge of wooden-ship builders. Although called shipworms, the holes and the shelly tubes they contain are actually made by a bivalve mollusc with a tiny shell that is used more as a drilling tool than for protection.

Holes made
by shipworms

Shelly tubes of
shipworm removed
from wood

Shipworms often
had a devastating
effect on early
sailing ships

Helmet shell

HIDE-AWAY HERMIT
The hermit crab, (right)
often seen in shallow water pools,
is not the natural inhabitant of
the shell in which it lives, as many
people think. This crab does not possess
a hard shell of its own, so it "borrows" an
empty mollusc shell and, as it grows, discards its
home in favour of a more spacious one.

Common
hermit crab

Scallop shell
embedded
in sponge

Roman
jar

COMFORTABLE ACCOMMODATION
Some shells can even be found
embedded in soft sections of natural sponge. This is often due to the
sponge overgrowing a dead shell, but
sometimes a mollusc will deliberately
select this soft site as its home, as in the
case of the scallop shell seen here.

IS IT A BIRD....?
The goose barnacles are crustaceans that can live,
attached by a stalk, to almost any object floating in
the sea - including the hulls of boats and ships. Goose
barnacles are socalled because of the similarity
between their shells and fleshy stalks and the white
head and black neck of a certain type of goose. It used
to be thought that the barnacles "grew up" and
turned into birds.

Goose barnacles

Barnacle
goose

Collecting shells

SHELL COLLECTING IS A POPULAR and satisfying hobby, and a walk along the beach may be enough to start a collection. It is sometimes necessary to collect living creatures, as their shells are often in better condition than those that have been tossed about by waves or weathered by the elements. Obtaining these may entail diving, or beachcombing at night. However, try to collect dead specimens unless you are actually studying the animal. Treat everything you touch with care, and, if you are overturning rocks or coral slabs to look underneath, make sure you return them to their original position. Take only what you need, and always leave some young specimens that will grow to produce future generations.

ON THE BEACH
Rock pools are often teeming with life, and shells that would normally only be found in deeper waters are sometimes stranded there. It pays to look closely, as many creatures seek the darkness and moisture found in rock crevices or underneath stones.

COLLECTING UNDERWATER
Collecting underwater reveals many shells in their natural habitats. You can use a snorkel in shallow waters, and, with proper training, scuba diving will open up a new world.

Plastic collecting bags

Mask and snorkel

TOOLS OF THE TRADE
A keen pair of eyes is the first thing needed by the collector, as living shells seldom display the bright colours seen in collections. A knife is useful for prising shells off rocks, and some kind of collecting bag is essential. Sieves with a range of mesh sizes enable you quickly to separate shells of different sizes.

Strong penknife

Shells, rocks, and weed separated from sand

Sieve for sorting small shells from sand

Tweezers

Sharp knife
or scalpel

Uncleaned
specimen

Magnifying
glasses

Cotton
buds

Cleaned
specimen

Identification
reference book

More elongated
shape and lack
of dark markings
between ribs

Clearly defined
markings
between ribs

Heavier shell
with more
angular shape

Dental tool
for cleaning

CLEANING SPECIMENS

It is usually best to clean the shells
fairly soon after they have been
collected. The animals can be removed from the shells by boiling the
specimen slowly, cooling it down
and then "winkling" out the insides
with a bent pin. The shells will
usually need to be soaked for a few
hours in a 50/50 solution of household
bleach and water, then scrubbed.

IDENTITY PARADE

Examining shells with a magnifying glass or microscope
will reveal details that will help to identify them
correctly; for example, the three shells shown above are
very similar but are in fact all separate species. Most
shells have a name by which experts can identify them,
and you will need to refer to specialist guides
to name your collection.

Old tooth-
brush for
scrubbing

Labels

STORING
AND CATALOGUING

When you are out
collecting, always take a
notebook and record as much
information as possible about
each animal. Later, you can write
up these details in a catalogue and
label your specimens with the page
number. Most shells fade when
exposed to light, so store them
in the dark. Shallow
drawers are useful for
most types of shell, and you
can use small boxes or glass
tubes to divide types within
drawers.

Transparent plastic
boxes and film tube
for storage

*Plastic boxes with
identification
labels
underneath*

*Locality
data*

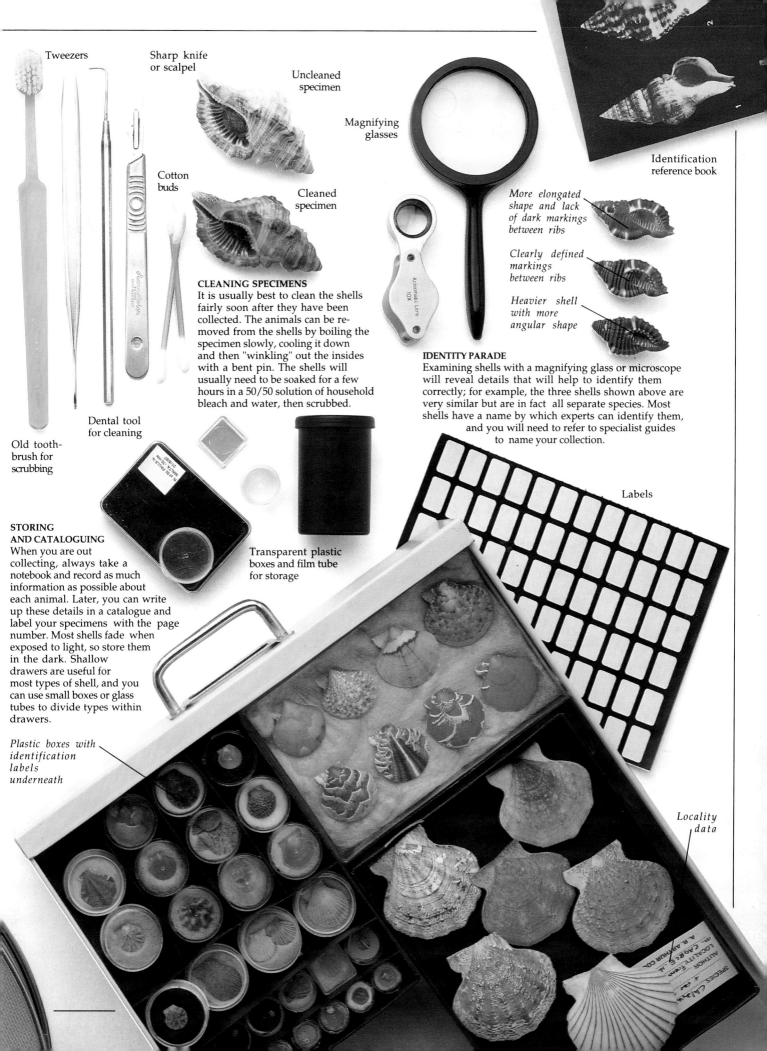

Index

Acknowledgements

Dorling Kindersley would like to thank:
David Attard (Malta), Andrew Clarke (British Antarctic Survey); Derek Coombes; Geoff Cox, Koën Fraussen (Belgium); Dr. Ray Ingle, Dr. Roger Lincoln, Colin McCarthy, Chris Owen, and Andrew Stimson of the British Museum (Natural History); Samuel Jones (Pearls) Ltd.; Sue Mennell; Alistair Moncur; José Maria Hernandez Otero (Spain); Tom and Celia Pain; Respectable Reptiles; Alan Seccombe; Dr. Francisco Garcia Talavera, Museum of Santa Cruz (Natural History); Ken Wye (Eaton's Shell Shop); John Youles.

Lynn Bresler for the index
Fred Ford and Mike Pilley of Radius Graphics
Karl Shone for special photography on pages 6-7 and 40-41
Jane Burton for special photography on page 59

Picture credits
(t=top, b=bottom, m=middle, l=left, r=right)
Doug Allan: 26
The Ancient Art & Architecture Collection: 44br
Heather Angel: 20, 25, 40tl & mr, 46tr, 54tl
Ardea London: 29tr, 35mr
Axel Poignant Archive: 39MR
BBC Hulton Picture Library: 37T&BL
The Bridgeman Art Library/Uffizi Gallery, Florence: 16
The Bridgeman Art Library/Alan Jacobs Gallery, London: 22tr
Bruce Coleman Ltd.: 7tr
Mary Evans Picture Library: 8, 11, 12, 15, 19br, 22br, 26tl, 28tl, 30tr, 34tl & mr, 36br, 50tl, 57 tl & mr, 59mr
The Kobal Collection/20th-Century

Fox: 14
National Museum of Wales: 38bl
Planet Earth Pictures/Seaphot: 19ml, 24br, 27, 42, 52tl, 53tm& bm, 58bl
Rothschild Estate: 30BR
Robert Harding Picture Library: 55bl 54, 56, 58

Illustrators: Will Giles, Sandra Pond: 21b; 35t; 43b;